Basic Sight Singing

Byron K. Yasui

Allen R. Trubitt

University of Hawaii at Manoa

Mayfield Publishing Co.
Mountain View, California

To our parents

Library of Congress Cataloging-in-Publication Data

Yasui, Byron K.
  Basic sight singing.

  1. Sight-singing.   I. Trubitt, Allen R.
II. Title.
MT870.Y35   1989   88–753239
ISBN 0–87484–880–6

Manufactured in the United States of America
10 9 8 7 6 5 4 3 2 1

Mayfield Publishing Company
1240 Villa Street
Mountain View, CA 94041

Sponsoring editor, Janet M. Beatty; Cover designer, Holly McLaughlin; Text designer/Typesetter, A-R Editions;
Printer and Binder, Bookcrafters.

Preface

We've designed this collection of rudimentary exercises to help beginners sight-sing. It is not a text for elementary music theory; it contains only enough prose to explain the exercises and to offer a few ideas about sight singing. We've written it especially for those college undergraduates who hope to become music majors but whose musical background is at a basic level.

To help serve students at this basic level, we've incorporated some distinctive features:

- All examples are short (4–10 measures). We feel that many short examples are better than fewer long ones. Because the most difficult part of sight singing is getting a proper start with a melody, a basic premise of this text is that establishing a routine procedure for getting oriented to the melody is of the highest importance. Short melodies allow maximum time to be spent in this critical orientation to new melodies (determining the key, scale, tempo, and certain essential reference pitches). The melodies are generally through-composed; recapitulations are avoided.

- Each chapter presents rhythmic exercises first, followed by pitch exercises, staff familiarization exercises, and melodies (solos and duets composed by the authors and examples from the literature). Some of the melodies from the literature have been transposed or otherwise adapted to the purpose of the text. All examples not attributed were composed by us.

- The duets provide a different musical experience from that typically offered in a sight-singing class—where one student sings and the rest of the class listens. To actively enlist the entire class, you may choose to have one student sing one line of a duet while the rest of the class sings the other.

- All melodies are within the range of an octave (with rare exceptions in the examples from the literature) to help students who have little experience in singing. Melodies are grouped by range (tonic to tonic or dominant to dominant) to draw the attention of the student to the importance of selecting a suitable pitch for the tonic.

- Solfège syllable letters are used along with scale degree numbers to represent pitches in Part I. You may decide to use one system, both, or another system altogether. Because of the differences that arise between various systems in the minor keys, only scale degree numbers are used in Part II, when the minor key is introduced.

- Exercises are very carefully graded. Rhythmic complexities and the various scale degrees are introduced gradually, and melodic skips are only to pitches of the tonic triad (with a few exceptions in the examples from the literature). Pitch is presented in successive levels of difficulty, with the emphasis on learning to hear the tones as scale degrees in relation to tonic pitch. Some exercises employ only scale degree number and solfège syllables to eliminate the distraction of rhythmic problems or staff notation. Next are exercises that show how these scale degrees are located on the staff, without a clef. Once students realize the connection between the scale degrees and the location of the notes on the staff, the matter of key and clef becomes less relevant. The melodic exercises are divided into two groups: melodies with the tonic in one staff position and melodies with the tonic in various staff positions. Consequently, a wide variety of key signatures are used from the beginning, but students understand that the critical factor is the location of the scale degrees on the staff.

- Rhythms are limited to subdivisions, that is, division of the beat into not more than four subdivisions in simple meters, and not more than six subdivisions in compound meters.

- Only treble and bass clefs are used, with ranges extending to two ledger lines above and below the staff.

- The text is neutral with regard to the various solfège systems, and there is no attempt to cultivate absolute pitch.

- Some exercises contain long rests and sustained notes to provide practice in counting and to allow a moment for the students to develop their ability to anticipate the next pitch.
- A convenient reference table of key signatures can be found on the inside back cover.

In addition, we've included in an instructor's manual many teaching suggestions and a list of many of the software programs currently available for sight-singing classes.

Acknowledgments

We wish to express appreciation and gratitude to our colleague, Professor Armand Russell, who tested these materials in class and made valuable suggestions for improving the text. We would also like to acknowledge our appreciation to the following reviewers of the text for their many excellent suggestions: Michael Arenson, University of Delaware; Robert I. Hurwitz, University of Oregon; Daniel Kazez, Wittenberg University; Samuel Magrill, Central State University; David Mallory, California State University at Chico; and John Scandrett, Indiana University of Pennsylvania.

Contents

Part I: Major Keys

Chapter 1
Rhythm. Simple and Compound Meters; Undivided Beats and Rests 3
Pitch. Tonic to Dominant 12
Examples from the Literature 29

Chapter 2
Rhythm. Simple Meter Only; Undivided and Divided Beats (÷ 2) 31
Pitch. Tonic to Tonic 34
Examples from the Literature 52

Chapter 3
Rhythm. Compound Meter Only; Undivided and Divided Beats (÷ 3) 54
Pitch. Dominant to Dominant 57
Examples from the Literature 75

Chapter 4: Summary of Part I
Rhythm. Simple and Compound Meters; Undivided and Divided Beats (÷ 2, ÷ 3), with Ties 77
Pitch. Tonic to Tonic; Dominant to Dominant 80
Examples from the Literature 87

Part II: Minor Keys

Chapter 5
Rhythm. Simple Meter Only; Subdivided Beats (÷ 4), without Ties 91
Pitch. Tonic to Tonic 95
Examples from the Literature 108

Chapter 6
Rhythm. Compound Meter Only; Subdivided Beats (÷ 6), without Ties .110
Pitch. Tonic to Tonic 116
Examples from the Literature 122

Chapter 7
Rhythm. Simple Meter Only; Subdivided Beats (÷ 4), with Ties 125
Pitch. Dominant to Dominant 130
Examples from the Literature 144

Chapter 8
Rhythm. Compound Meter Only; Subdivided Beats (÷ 6), with Ties 146
Pitch. Dominant to Dominant 152
Examples from the Literature 158

Chapter 9: Summary of Part II
Rhythm. Simple and Compound Meters; Subdivided Beats (÷ 4, ÷ 6), with Ties 160
Pitch. Dominant to Dominant; Tonic to Tonic 164
Examples from the Literature 171

Part III: Supplementary Exercises

Chapter 10: Additional Exercises in Major and Minor Keys

Rhythm Exercises 175
Pitch Exercises 178
Examples from the Literature 183

Part I

Chapter 1

RHYTHM
simple and compound meters;
undivided beats and rests

PITCH
tonic to dominant

Rhythm

Beat: A pulse, heard or felt at regular intervals, usually 60–150 times per minute.
Basic Duration: The time that elapses between the beats.
Tempo: The rate at which the beats occur.
Meter: A recurrent grouping of beats into regular patterns, usually of two, three, four, or six beats. Each grouping is called a *measure* or *bar* and is indicated by a vertical *bar line* on the staff.

Music consists of sounds and silences organized by regular pulses or beats. Music notation consists of a set of symbols called *notes* and *rests*; each symbol represents a particular duration of sound or silence.

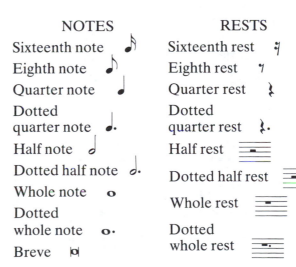

The breve is sometimes called *double whole note*. The whole rest may be used to indicate a silence of one measure's duration, whatever the

3

time signature. (The time signature is explained later in this chapter.)

Eighth notes and sixteenth notes may be written with *flags* or with *beams* (see diagram), but there should be no difference in the manner of performance.

flags   beam   flags   beams

A dot following a note or a rest increases the duration by half. Thus, a dotted whole note has a duration equal to the combined durations of a whole note and a half note.

$$o\cdot = o + d$$

The time elapsing between the pulses, or beats, is represented by one of the notes shown in the list on page 3. For each piece, the composer decides which note value to use for this purpose.

Notes and rests have fixed relative values. The following list shows the notes in order of increasing length, the shortest at the top. Each undotted note in the series has half the duration of the next larger value. The same principle applies to dotted notes.

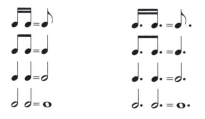

Therefore, if a quarter note is used to represent one basic duration, the half note represents two basic durations. From this you can see that the same rhythm can be written in different ways, de-

pending on which of the note values is chosen to represent the basic duration.

1. The beat represented by ♪

2. The beat represented by ♩

3. The beat represented by 𝅝

The composer decides which of these notations to use. The factors governing that decision are beyond the scope of this book. The performer learns which note represents the beat from the *meter signature,* or *time signature,* which consists of two numbers written one above the other on the staff before any notes appear. Thus, the previous examples would look like this:

1.

2.

3.

In simple meters, the lower number indicates the note value used to represent the beat, and the upper number indicates the regular grouping of the beats into a pattern typically consisting of two, three, or four beats. The location of the bar lines also reflects the grouping.

Some time signatures, representing what are called *compound meters,* may be interpreted differently; these will be discussed later in this chapter. In some exercises in this book, the note value representing the beat is indicated by a note written above the first measure of the music.

The following time signatures are used in this text:

$$\frac{3}{8} \quad \frac{4}{8} \quad \frac{2}{4} \quad \frac{3}{4} \quad \frac{4}{4} \quad \frac{2}{2} \quad \frac{3}{2} \quad \frac{4}{2} \quad \frac{6}{8} \quad \frac{9}{8} \quad \frac{12}{8} \quad \frac{6}{4}$$

Two other symbols are also used: $\mathbf{C} = \frac{4}{4}$ and $\mathbf{\cent} = \frac{2}{2}$.

Rhythmic Exercises

The rhythmic exercises in this book should be practiced and performed using this routine:

1. Glance through the exercise to see if there are any unfamiliar notational symbols or other problems. Understand the notation thoroughly before you begin.

2. Examine the time signature to see how the exercise will be counted, that is, what note value represents the beat. In all exercises and examples in this chapter and in certain exercises later in the book, you will see a note value above the first measure, indicating the note representing the beat. Your counting should be gauged by this note value. Find a tempo at which you can perform the exercise while counting the designated beats. Avoid "converting" to a more familiar meter; for example, do not change $\frac{2}{2}$ to $\frac{4}{4}$.

3. Glance again through the exercise to see how difficult the rhythms are. Choose a tempo that will allow you to perform the rhythms accurately while counting the beats as indicated in step 2.

4. Establish the tempo by conducting or tapping the beat with your toe or your finger. Your teacher may indicate a preference.

5. Maintaining a steady beat, intone the rhythm, using the syllable *ta* or any other method recommended by your teacher.

6. If you make a mistake, try to recover without stopping, going back, or adding extra beats.

Exercises

Often, the first beat of each measure receives a slight emphasis, although this emphasis is usually rather subtle. However, not every piece begins with the first beat of the measure; for example, exercise 4 begins on the third beat of the measure. Any note (or notes) that precedes the first full measure of a piece is known as the *upbeat(s)* or the *anacrusis*. Sometimes a piece beginning with an upbeat will end with an incomplete measure, but there are many instances where that does not happen.

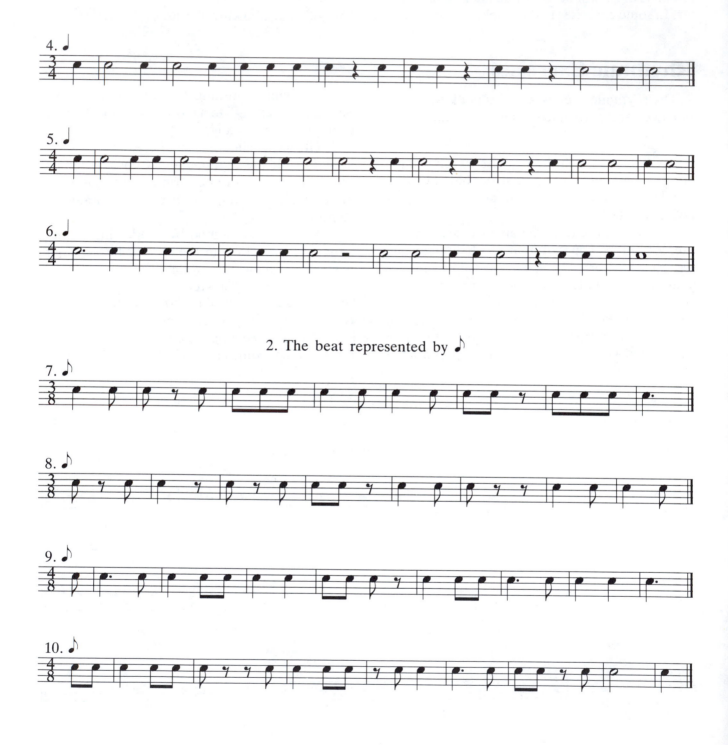

2. The beat represented by ♪

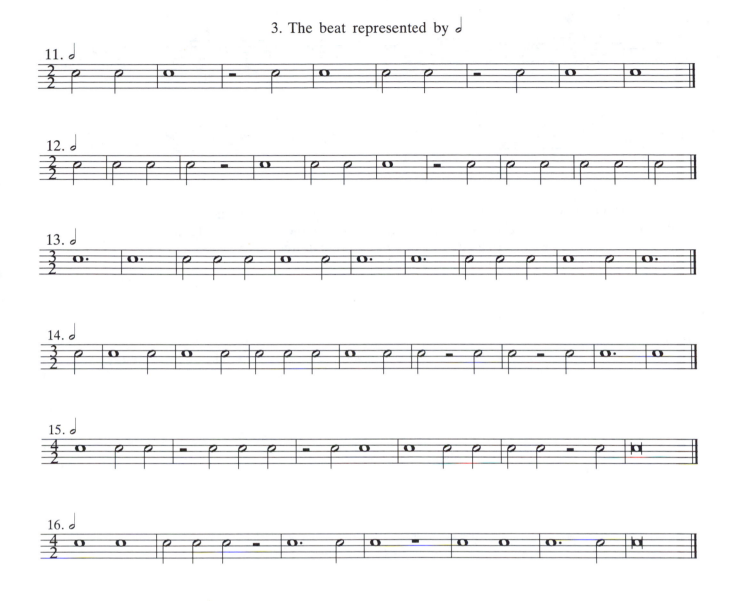

4. The beat represented by ♩.

Pieces written in $\frac{3}{8}$, $\frac{3}{4}$, $\frac{6}{4}$, $\frac{6}{8}$, $\frac{9}{8}$, and $\frac{12}{8}$ (compound meters) may not always follow the rule given earlier for interpreting time signatures. If the tempo of the meter is quick, do not count the note value shown in the lower number of the time signature. Instead, count the measure in groups of three beats (notice that the upper number is divisible by three). Thus, in exercise 17, it is more convenient to count only two beats to the measure

than to count six quicker beats.

In this book, the note written over the first measure will tell you how the example should be counted.

The durations of two or more notes may be combined by means of a *tie*. The result is a single, uninterrupted tone whose length is the sum of all the durations of the tied notes. Only the first note of a group of tied notes is articulated. For instance, the tie is needed to indicate a note equal to three dotted quarter notes.

Exercises with Ties

Reminder: When two or more notes are tied together, only the first note is articulated.

1. The beat represented by ♩

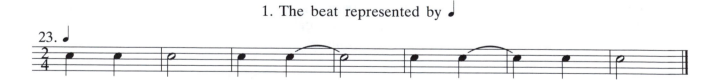

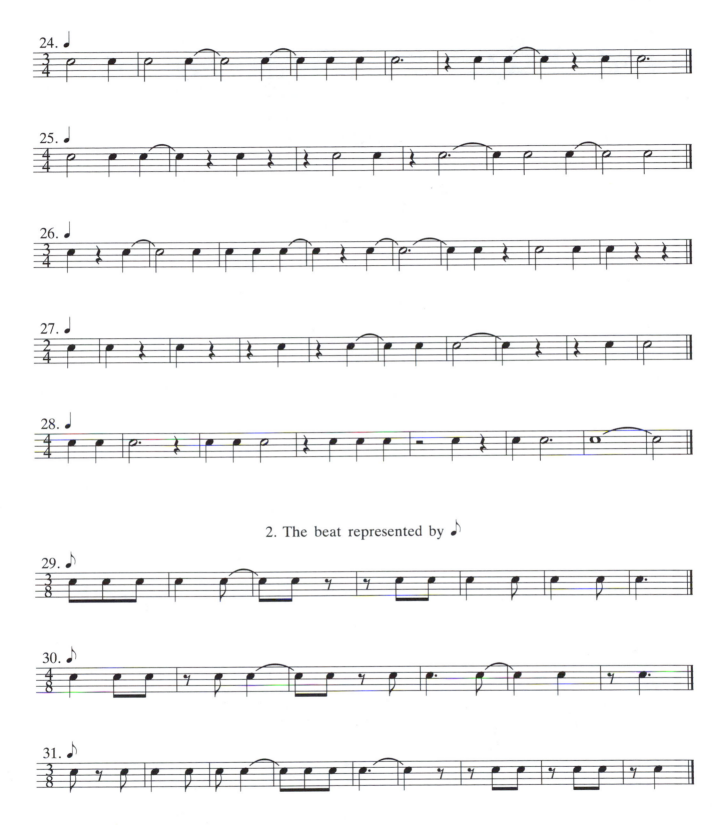

3. The beat represented by ♩

4. The beat represented by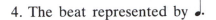

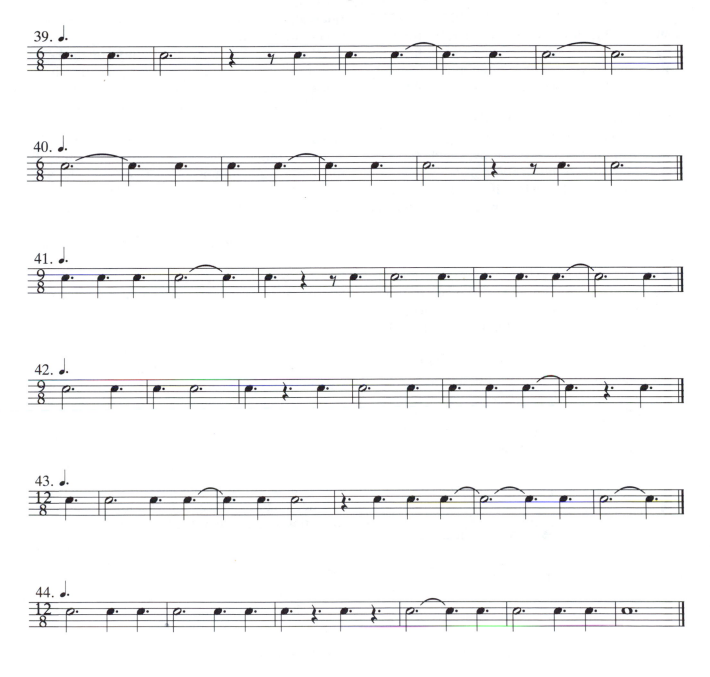

Pitch (range: tonic to dominant)

Tonic: The first note of the scale. The central tone in a piece. It is usually implied in the first few notes of a melody and most often, but not always, is heard at the end, where it gives a sense of arrival at a goal.

Major Scale: The pattern of pitches heard by playing the white keys on the piano beginning on C and ascending one octave, or by singing through the syllables *do re mi fa sol la ti do*. The major scale consists of whole steps between all consecutive scale degrees, except between 3 and 4 (*mi* and *fa*) and between 7 and 8 (*ti* and *do*), which are half steps.

Scale Degrees: The notes of the scale in numerical order. The tonic is the first scale degree, and the other tones are numbered in order of ascending pitch. The first, the third, the fifth, and the eighth scale degrees are basic reference tones used in sight singing.

Solfège or Solfeggio: A method used for teaching sight singing employing a traditional set of syllables. Each tone of the scale is assigned a syllable. The student learns to associate the syllable with the specific pitch. The syllables correspond to the scale degree numbers as follows:

do	*re*	*mi*	*fa*	*sol*	*la*	*ti*	*do*
1	2	3	4	5	6	7	8

In Part I of this book, the two methods of identifying pitches will be combined in this abbreviated form:

d/1   r/2   m/3   f/4   s/5   l/6   t/7   d/8

Interval: The distance or difference in pitch between two tones.

Half Step: The distance from one note on the keyboard to the next consecutive key, whether it is black or white. The distance between scale degrees 3 and 4 (*mi* and *fa*) and between 7 and 8 (*ti* and *do*).

Whole Step: The interval of two consecutive half steps, as found between the first two notes of the major scale, *do* and *re* (first and second scale degrees).

Key Signature: A series of sharps or flats written at the beginning of a piece of music to indicate the tonic pitch and the scale to be employed. In this text, key signatures refer only to major or minor keys. A complete list of these signatures for all major and minor keys is found on the back inside cover.

Before you begin to sing from staff notation, you must establish in your ear the basic patterns of the various scale degrees. In this chapter, we will limit ourselves to the first five degrees of the major scale. We will begin with only three tones, gradually adding others. In the Scale Degree Number / Solfège exercises, the tones are presented as a series of numbers, without notes. Practice singing these exercises until you can sing the series fluently, at a steady tempo.

Level 1 Exercises: scale degrees 1 2 3 / d r m (stepwise motion only)

Scale Degree Number

a.   1 2 3 2 3 2 1 2 1 2 3 2 3

b.   2 1 2 3 2 1 2 1 2 3 2 3 2

c.   3 2 1 2 1 2 3 2 3 2 1 2 3

d.   2 1 2 3 2 3 2 1 2 1 2 3 2

Solfège

a.   d r m r m r d r d r m r m

b.   r d r m r d r d r m r m r

c.   m r d r d r m r m r d r m

d.   r d r m r m r d r d r m r

Scale Degree Number (continued)

e. 1 2 3 2 3 2 1 2 1 2 3 2 1

f. 3 2 1 2 1 2 3 2 3 2 3 2 1

g. 1 2 3 2 3 2 3 2 1 2 1 2 3

h. 1 2 3 2 1 2 1 2 3 2 3 2 1

i. 2 3 2 1 2 1 2 3 2 3 2 1 2

j. 3 2 1 2 3 2 3 2 1 2 1 2 3

k. 2 3 2 3 2 1 2 1 2 3 2 1 2

l. 3 2 3 2 1 2 1 2 3 2 3 2 1

Solfège (continued)

e. d r m r m r d r d r m r d

f. m r d r d r m r m r m r d

g. d r m r m r m r d r d r m

h. d r m r d r d r m r m r d

i. r m r d r d r m r m r d r

j. m r d r m r m r d r d r m

k. r m r m r d r d r m r d r

l. m r m r d r d r m r m r d

Both treble and bass clefs will be used throughout this text. If you are not very familiar with these clefs, don't worry; fluency will come with practice. In fact, for many of our exercises the clef is relatively unimportant. What is most important is the position of the tonic. Once the tonic is located, the other scale degrees fall logically into place. If the first degree of the scale falls on a line, the second degree will be on the adjacent space above. If the first scale degree is on a line, the third and the fifth degrees will be on the next two lines above. If the tonic is on a space, the third and the fifth degrees will be on the next two spaces above.

In the following exercises, no clef is given; 1 / d indicates the position of the tonic on the staff.

These exercises should be done in two ways: first, recite in a fluent fashion the scale degree number or solfège syllable that each note represents; second, sing in a fluent fashion, the notes as pitches, using the appropriate scale degree numbers or solfège syllables. Do not write the scale degree numbers or solfège syllables under the notes. These exercises are intended to be used repeatedly, as needed, especially for review purposes.

Notes on the Staff

Tonic is on the first line below the staff.

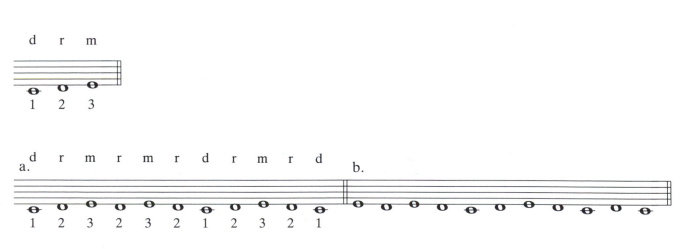

c.   d.

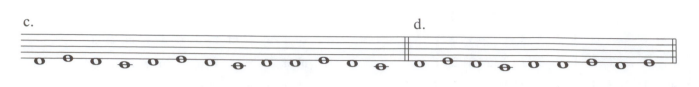

Melodies

Many different keys are used in this text. If you are not already familiar with all the major key signatures, you will want to learn them as quickly as you can,* but this need not delay your progress in sight singing. In our first exercises, the tonic always lies on the first line below the staff. *Recite* the scale degree number or syllable of each note, then *sing* the melody, using the same numbers or syllables. Maintain a steady pace.

Becoming a good sight singer is partly a matter of developing appropriate habits. It is very important to have an established routine before you begin. You should always take the following steps before you begin to sight sing:

1. Sing the tonic and a scalelike pattern, such as 1 2 3 4 5 / d r m f s. If this is easy for you, just sing 1 3 4 / d m s, but don't begin singing with only the tonic in your ear; you *must* have other pitches in mind as well. Vocalizing the scale helps to develop familiarity with the feeling of singing particular pitches. A glance through the melody you are about to sing will allow you to anticipate common problems: melodic skips, dotted rhythms, ties, and so on.

2. With the key established, tap the beat to feel the tempo. Gauge your tempo by the quickest notes. Imagine how fast they will sound and gauge your speed accordingly.

Tonic is on the first line below the staff.
Note: Not all melodies begin on the tonic.

45.

46.

47.

See the back inside cover for information on key signatures.

In these exercises, you must determine the key to know the position of the tonic on the staff. On the back inside cover, you will find a list of major and minor keys with their key signatures.

Duets

The duets may be sung by the entire class divided into equal parts or by a single voice on one part and the rest of the class on the other. In the latter case, the class must sing softly enough to allow the solo voice to be heard.

As you first sing the duets, your attention will be mainly on performing your own part correctly, but as you become more confident in your singing, try to notice what the other part is doing and how the two parts interrelate.

Note: In this book, when the final pitch of a melody is a pitch other than tonic, the appropriate scale degree indication will be placed above or below the final pitch. Refer to exercise 55: The m / 3 above the final pitch of the upper voice indicates that that pitch is *mi* or scale degree number 3.

Level 2 Exercises: scale degrees 1 3 5 / d m s

<table>
<tr><td>

Scale Degree Number

a. 1 3 5 3 5 3 1 3 1 5 3 1 5

b. 3 5 1 5 3 1 3 1 5 3 5 1 3

c. 5 1 3 1 5 3 1 5 1 3 1 5 3

d. 1 3 5 1 5 1 3 1 3 5 3 1 5

e. 3 1 5 1 3 5 1 3 1 5 1 3 5

f. 1 5 3 1 5 1 3 5 3 1 5 3 1

g. 1 3 5 1 3 5 3 1 5 1 3 5 1

h. 5 3 1 5 1 3 1 5 3 1 5 1 3

i. 5 1 3 5 3 1 3 1 5 1 5 3 1

j. 3 5 1 3 1 5 1 3 5 1 3 1 5

k. 3 1 5 3 5 1 3 1 3 5 1 5 3

l. 5 1 3 5 1 3 1 3 5 3 5 3 1

</td><td>

Solfège

a. d m s m s m d m d s m d s

b. m s d s m d m d s m s d m

c. s d m d s m d s d m d s m

d. d m s d s d m d m s m d s

e. m d s d m s d m d s d m s

f. d s m d s d m s m d s m d

g. d m s d m s m d s d m s d

h. s m d s d m d s m d s d m

i. s d m s m d m d s d s m d

j. m s d m d s d m s d m d s

k. m d s d s d m d m s d s m

l. s d m s d m d m s m s m d

</td></tr>
</table>

Notes on the Staff

Tonic is on the first space.

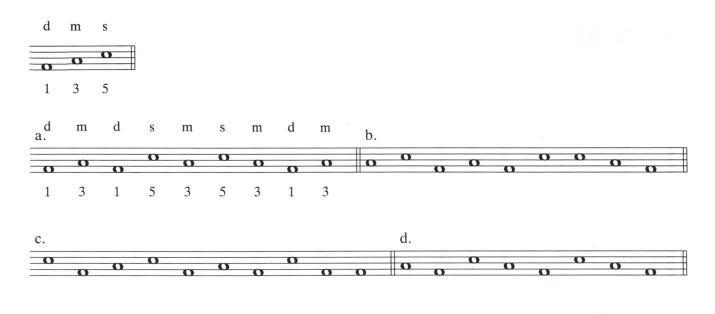

Melodies

Tonic is on the first space.

18   Chapter 1

Tonic is in various positions.

Duets

Level 3 Exercises: scale degrees 1 2 3 5 / d r m s

<table>
<tr><td>

Scale Degree Number

a. 1 2 3 2 3 5 1 5 1 2 5 3 1

b. 5 1 2 5 3 1 5 1 3 2 1 5 3

c. 3 2 5 1 3 1 2 3 1 5 3 1 5

d. 5 1 2 5 3 2 5 1 3 1 5 3 2

e. 1 3 2 5 3 1 5 1 2 3 5 1 2

f. 3 1 5 1 2 3 2 5 1 3 1 5 3

g. 3 5 1 3 1 5 3 2 5 1 5 1 3

h. 3 1 5 3 2 1 5 1 3 5 1 3 2

i. 3 2 5 1 3 1 2 5 3 5 1 2 5

j. 5 1 3 5 1 3 2 1 5 1 2 5 3

k. 3 5 1 2 3 1 5 1 3 5 5 3 2 5

l. 1 3 5 1 2 5 1 3 2 5 3 1 2

</td><td>

Solfège

a. d r m r m s d s d r s m d

b. s d r s m d s d m r d s m

c. m r s d m d r m d s m d s

d. s d r s m r s d m d s m r

e. d m r s m d s d r m s d r

f. m d s d r m r s d m d s m

g. m s d m d s m r s d s d m

h. m d s m r d s d m s d m r

i. m r s d m d r s m s d r s

j. s d m s d m r d s d r s m

k. m s d r m d s d m s m r s

l. d m s d r s d m r s m d r

</td></tr>
</table>

Notes on the Staff

Tonic is on the fourth line.

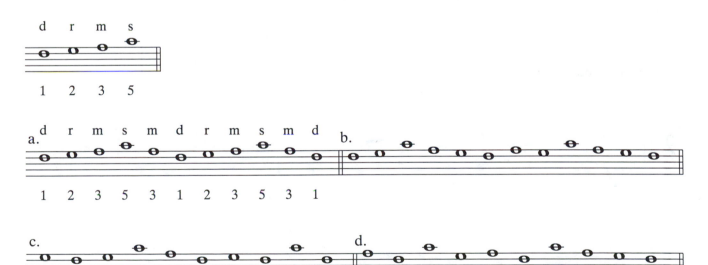

Melodies

Tonic is on the fourth line.

Tonic is in various positions.

72.

73.

Duets

74.

75.
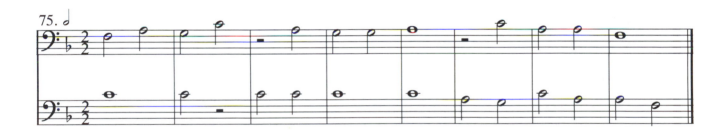

Level 4 Exercises: scale degrees 1 3 4 5 / d m f s

Scale Degree Number	Solfège
a. 1 3 4 5 3 1 5 4 5 3 1 5 4	a. d m f s m d s f s m d s f
b. 1 3 4 5 1 5 3 5 4 3 5 3 4	b. d m f s d s m s f m s m f
c. 5 1 3 4 1 5 3 1 5 4 3 5 1	c. s d m f d s m d s f m s d
d. 1 5 3 5 4 1 3 1 3 4 1 5 3	d. d s m s f d m d m f d s m
e. 3 5 4 1 3 4 1 5 3 1 5 3 4	e. m s f d m f d s m d s m f
f. 1 3 4 5 3 1 5 4 1 3 5 1 3	f. d m f s m d s f d m s d m
g. 5 1 3 4 1 5 4 1 3 1 5 4 3	g. ꞏs d m f d s f d m d s f m
h. 1 3 5 4 1 5 3 4 1 5 1 3 5	h. d m s f d s m f d s d m d
i. 3 4 1 5 3 1 5 4 3 5 1 5 4	i. m f d s m d s f m s d s f
j. 5 1 3 4 1 5 4 1 3 5 5 3 4 1	j. s d m f d s f d m s m f d
k. 3 1 3 4 5 3 1 5 4 1 3 5 1	k. m d m f s m d s f d m s d
l. 5 4 1 3 1 5 3 4 1 3 5 3 1	l. s f d m d s m f d m s m d

Notes on the Staff

Tonic is on the third line.

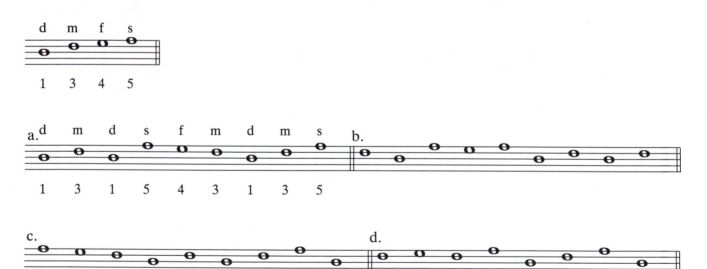

Melodies

Tonic is on the third line.

Tonic is in various positions.

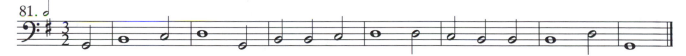

Duets

Level 5 Exercises: scale degrees 1 2 3 4 5 / d r m f s (stepwise motion only)

Scale Degree Number	Solfège
a. 1 2 3 2 3 4 5 4 3 4 3 2 3	a. d r m r m f s f m f m r m
b. 3 2 1 2 1 2 3 4 3 4 5 4 3	b. m r d r d r m f m f s f m
c. 2 3 2 3 4 5 4 3 4 3 2 1 2	c. r m r m f s f m f m r d r
d. 5 4 5 4 3 2 1 2 1 2 3 2 3	d. s f s f m r d r d r m r m
e. 1 2 3 4 3 4 5 4 3 2 3 2 1	e. d r m f m f s f m r m r d
f. 2 3 2 1 2 3 4 5 4 3 2 1 2	f. r m r d r m f s f m r d r
g. 2 1 2 3 4 5 4 3 2 1 2 3 2	g. r d r m f s f m r d r m r
h. 1 2 3 2 3 4 5 4 3 4 3 2 1	h. d r m r m f s f m f m r d
i. 3 2 3 2 1 2 1 2 3 4 5 4 5	i. m r m r d r d r m f s f s
j. 2 1 2 3 4 3 4 5 4 3 2 3 2	j. r d r m f m f s f m r m r
k. 3 4 5 4 3 4 3 2 1 2 1 2 3	k. m f s f m f m r d r d r m
l. 3 2 3 4 3 4 5 4 3 2 3 2 1	l. m r m f m f s f m r m r d

Notes on the Staff

Tonic is on the fifth line.

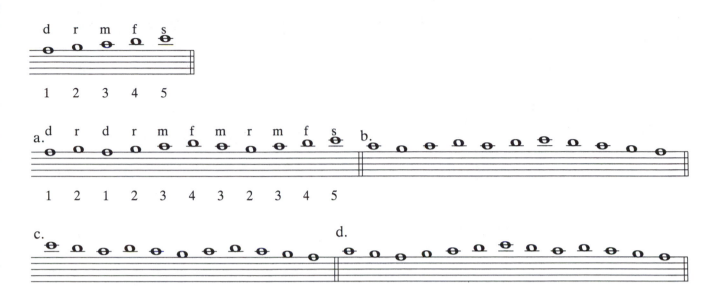

Melodies

Tonic is on the fifth line.

Tonic is in various positions.

m/3

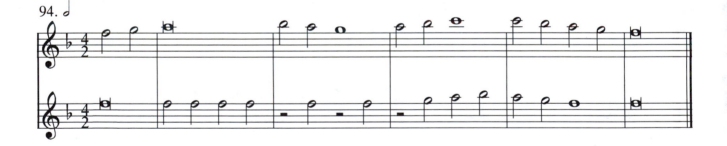

Duets

Level 6 Exercises: scale degrees 1 2 3 4 5 / d r m f s (steps and skips)

<table>
<tr><td colspan="2">Scale Degree Number</td><td colspan="2">Solfège</td></tr>
<tr><td>a.</td><td>1 2 3 5 4 1 3 2 3 4 1 2 5</td><td>a.</td><td>d r m s f d m r m f d r s</td></tr>
<tr><td>b.</td><td>3 5 4 1 2 3 1 5 3 1 5 4 3</td><td>b.</td><td>m s f d r m d s m d s f m</td></tr>
<tr><td>c.</td><td>2 3 2 1 2 5 4 3 4 1 3 2 5</td><td>c.</td><td>r m r d r s f m f d m r s</td></tr>
<tr><td>d.</td><td>1 5 3 4 1 5 4 1 3 2 5 1 2</td><td>d.</td><td>d s m f d s f d m r s d r</td></tr>
<tr><td>e.</td><td>5 1 3 2 5 4 1 3 4 1 2 5 3</td><td>e.</td><td>s d m r s f d m f d r s m</td></tr>
<tr><td>f.</td><td>3 1 5 4 3 1 2 5 3 4 1 3 2</td><td>f.</td><td>m d s f m d r s m f d m r</td></tr>
<tr><td>g.</td><td>3 2 5 4 3 1 2 5 3 4 1 2 5</td><td>g.</td><td>m r s f m d r s m f d r s</td></tr>
<tr><td>h.</td><td>3 1 2 5 4 1 3 2 1 3 4 1 5</td><td>h.</td><td>m d r s f d m r d m f d s</td></tr>
<tr><td>i.</td><td>1 5 3 4 1 3 2 5 4 1 2 5 3</td><td>i.</td><td>d s m f d m r s f d r s m</td></tr>
<tr><td>j.</td><td>3 1 2 5 3 4 1 5 4 3 1 5 3</td><td>j.</td><td>m d r s m f d s f m d s m</td></tr>
<tr><td>k.</td><td>1 3 2 5 3 4 5 1 3 2 5 1 2</td><td>k.</td><td>d m r s m f s d m r s d r</td></tr>
<tr><td>l.</td><td>1 5 4 1 3 2 1 5 1 2 5 3 1</td><td>l.</td><td>d s f d m r d s d r s m d</td></tr>
</table>

Notes on the Staff

Tonic is on the second space below the staff.

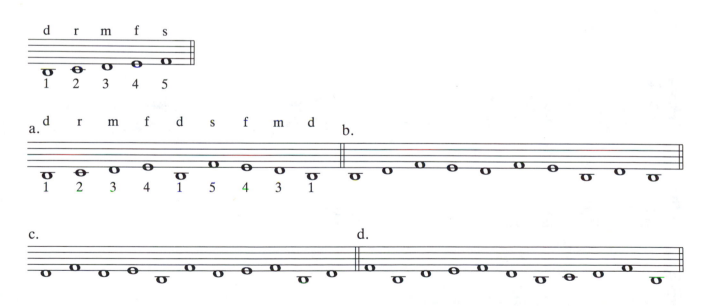

Melodies

Tonic is on the second space below the staff.

Tonic is in various positions.

103.

Duets

104.

s/5

105.

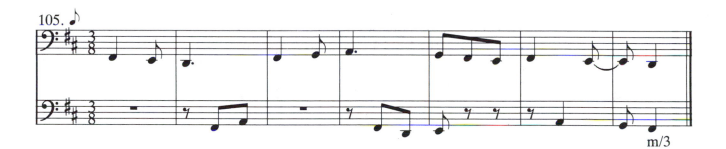

m/3

Examples from the Literature

106.   German Folk Song

107.   Carulli

108.
H. Finck

German Folk Song
109.

110.
Soriano

Carissimi
111.

16th Century
112.

Chapter **2**

RHYTHM

simple meter only;
undivided and divided beats (÷ 2)

PITCH

tonic to tonic

Rhythm

Simple Division: Division of the beat into two equal parts.
Simple Meter: A meter in which the beat, or basic duration, is divided into two equal parts. For example, in $\frac{2}{4}$ or $\frac{3}{4}$, the quarter note representing the beat may be divided into two eighths.

Exercises without Ties

1.

2.

3.

4.

5.

6.

7.

8.

Exercises with Ties

9.

Pitch (range: tonic to tonic)

Level 1 Exercises: scale degrees 1 5 8 / d s d̄

Note: A dash above the d represents the high *do,* as distinguished from the low *do.*

Scale Degree Number

a. 1 5 8 5 8 1 5 1 8 5 1 8 1
b. 5 1 5 8 1 8 5 1 8 5 8 1 5
c. 1 8 5 1 5 1 8 5 8 1 5 1 8
d. 5 8 1 5 1 8 5 1 5 8 1 5 8
e. 8 1 5 1 5 8 5 1 8 5 1 8 1
f. 1 5 8 1 8 5 1 5 1 8 5 1 5
g. 5 1 5 8 1 5 1 5 8 1 8 5 1
h. 1 8 1 5 8 1 5 8 5 1 5 1 8
i. 8 5 1 8 5 1 5 8 1 5 1 8 5
j. 8 1 5 1 8 5 8 1 5 1 5 8 1
k. 5 1 8 5 8 1 5 8 1 8 5 1 5
l. 1 8 1 5 8 1 5 1 8 5 8 5 1

Solfège

a. d s d̄ s d̄ d s d̄ d s d d̄ d
b. s d s d̄ d d̄ s d d̄ s d̄ d s
c. d d̄ s d s d d̄ s d̄ d s d d̄
d. s d̄ d s d d̄ s d s d̄ d s d̄
e. d̄ d s d s d̄ s d d̄ s d d̄ d
f. d s d̄ d d̄ s d s d d̄ s d s
g. s d s d̄ d s d s d̄ d d̄ s d
h. d d̄ d s d̄ d s d̄ s d s d d̄
i. d̄ s d d̄ s d s d̄ d s d d̄ s
j. d̄ d s d d̄ s d̄ d s d s d̄ d
k. s d d̄ s d̄ d s d̄ d d̄ s d s
l. d d̄ d s d̄ d s d d̄ s d̄ s d

Notes on the Staff

Tonic is on the third space.

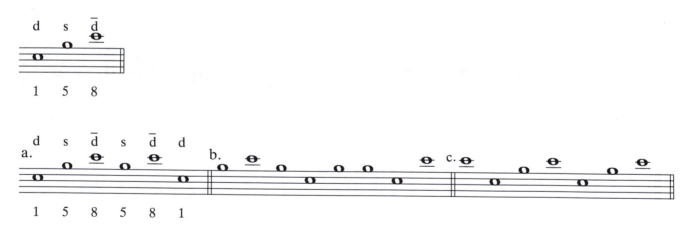

Melodies

Tonic is on the third space.

Tonic is in various positions.

23.

24.

25.

Duets

26.

27.

Level 2 Exercises: scale degrees 1 3 5 8 / d m s d̄

Scale Degree Number

a. 1 3 5 8 5 1 3 8 3 8 1 8 5
b. 8 5 1 3 5 1 8 3 5 8 3 5 1
c. 3 5 1 8 5 1 3 8 1 5 3 8 3
d. 8 3 5 1 3 8 5 1 5 8 3 1 8
e. 5 3 8 1 3 5 1 8 3 8 5 1 5
f. 3 8 1 5 3 1 8 5 3 5 8 1 3
g. 3 1 8 3 5 3 8 1 3 5 1 8 3
h. 5 1 5 8 3 8 1 5 3 1 8 3 5
i. 8 1 3 8 5 1 5 8 3 1 5 3 8
j. 3 8 3 5 1 8 3 1 5 8 1 5 3
k. 1 5 3 8 5 3 8 1 5 3 1 5 8
l. 5 8 1 8 3 8 3 1 5 8 5 3 1

Solfège

a. d m s d̄ s d m d̄ m d̄ d d̄ s
b. d̄ s d m s d d̄ m s d̄ m s d
c. m s d d̄ s d m d̄ d s m d̄ m
d. d̄ m s d m d̄ s d s d̄ m d d̄
e. s m d̄ d m s d̄ d̄ m d̄ s d s
f. m d̄ d s m d d̄ s m s d̄ d m
g. m d d̄ m s m d̄ d m s d d̄ m
h. s d s d̄ m d̄ d s m d d̄ m s
i. d̄ d m d̄ s d s d̄ m d s m d̄
j. m d̄ m s d d̄ m d s d̄ d s m
k. d s m d̄ s m d̄ d s m d s d̄
l. s d̄ d d̄ m d̄ m d s d̄ s m d

Notes on the Staff

Tonic is on the second line.

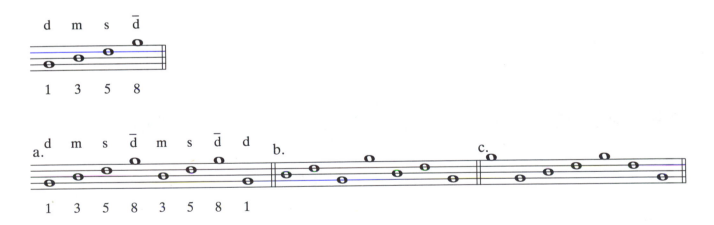

Melodies

Tonic is on the second line.

Tonic is in various positions.

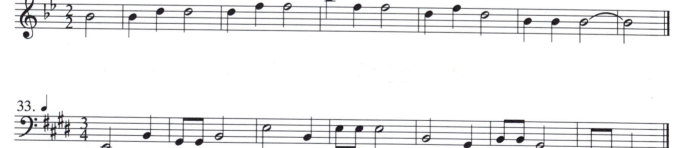

34.

35.

Duets

36.

37.

Level 3 Exercises: scale degrees 1 2 3 5 8 / d r m s d̄

Scale Degree Number

a. 1 2 3 5 8 1 3 2 8 1 5 3 2
b. 3 2 5 1 2 8 5 3 8 1 5 3 8
c. 1 5 3 2 8 1 5 1 2 8 3 2 5
d. 5 8 1 3 2 5 1 2 8 3 5 1 2
e. 3 2 8 5 1 2 3 8 1 5 3 2 8
f. 1 3 5 8 1 3 2 1 5 1 2 3 8
g. 3 2 8 5 1 5 1 2 8 3 1 2 5
h. 1 5 3 2 8 1 2 5 8 3 1 5 8
i. 3 8 5 1 2 5 3 2 8 3 2 5 1
j. 5 3 2 5 8 1 2 3 1 8 3 2 5
k. 3 5 1 2 8 1 3 2 5 8 1 5 3
l. 8 5 3 2 5 1 2 8 3 5 1 2 8

Solfège

a. d r m s d̄ d̄ m r d̄ d̄ s m r
b. m r s d r d̄ s m d̄ d̄ s m d̄
c. d s m r d̄ d̄ s d r d̄ m r s
d. s d̄ d m r s d r d̄ m s d r
e. m r d̄ s d r m d̄ d̄ s m r d̄
f. d m s d̄ d̄ m r d s d r m d̄
g. m r d̄ s d s d r d̄ m d r s
h. d s m r d̄ d̄ r s d̄ m d s d̄
i. m d̄ s d r s m r d̄ m r s d
j. s m r s d̄ d̄ r m d d̄ m r s
k. m s d r d̄ d̄ m r s d̄ d̄ s m
l. d̄ s m r s d r d̄ m s d r d̄

Notes on the Staff

Tonic is on the first line.

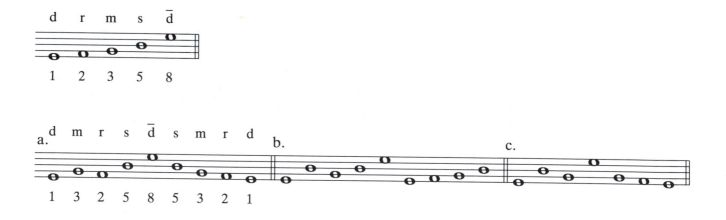

Melodies

Tonic is on the first line.

Tonic is in various positions.

44.

45.

Duets

46.

47.

Level 4 Exercises: scale degrees 1 2 3 5 6 8 / d r m s l d̄

Scale Degree Number

a. 1 2 3 5 6 8 5 3 2 5 1 2 8

b. 3 1 2 5 6 1 8 3 2 5 8 5 6

c. 5 6 1 8 3 2 8 1 5 1 5 6 3

d. 1 5 3 2 8 1 5 6 3 1 2 5 6

e. 5 6 8 1 3 2 5 1 2 5 6 8 3

f. 3 5 1 8 5 6 1 3 2 1 2 5 6

g. 1 5 6 3 2 8 1 2 5 6 8 3 2

h. 5 3 1 2 8 5 6 3 8 3 2 1 5

i. 8 3 5 6 3 1 2 5 3 2 8 5 6

j. 3 2 5 1 8 5 6 1 2 5 3 8 1

k. 5 6 8 3 2 5 1 2 8 5 6 3 2

l. 1 3 2 5 6 8 3 1 2 8 5 6 3

Solfège

a. d r m s l d̄ s m r s d r d̄

b. m d r s l d d̄ m r s d̄ s l

c. s l d d̄ m r d̄ d s d s l m

d. d s m r d̄ d s l m d r s l

e. s l d̄ d m r s d r s l d̄ m

f. m s d d̄ s l d m r d r s l

g. d s l m r d̄ d r s l d̄ m r

h. s m d r d̄ s l m d̄ m r d s

i. d̄ m s l m d r s m r d̄ s l

j. m r s d d̄ s l d r s m d̄ d

k. s l d̄ m r s d r d̄ s l m r

l. d m r s l d̄ m d r d̄ s l m

Notes on the Staff

Tonic is on the second space.

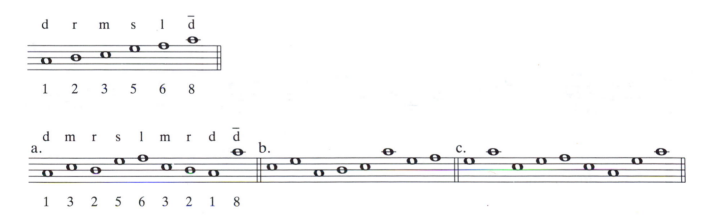

Melodies

Tonic is on the second space.

Tonic is in various positions.

54.

55.

56.

Duets

57.

s/5

58

Level 5 Exercises: scale degrees 1 2 3 5 6 7 8 / d r m s l t d̄

Scale Degree Number

a.   1 2 3 5 6 7 8 7 5 6 3 2 1
b.   3 5 6 1 2 8 7 6 3 5 1 2 8
c.   5 1 8 7 3 2 5 6 1 8 5 6 3
d.   8 5 6 1 2 5 3 2 5 6 8 7 3
e.   1 3 2 5 6 8 7 3 1 2 5 6 7
f.   3 1 2 5 6 1 8 7 3 5 1 3 2
g.   5 6 8 7 3 1 2 5 3 2 5 8 7
h.   3 5 6 8 1 2 8 7 6 3 5 3 2
i.   3 1 2 5 6 8 3 8 7 3 2 1 5
j.   8 5 6 3 2 1 8 7 3 1 2 5 6
k.   3 5 6 1 8 7 3 2 5 1 2 8 5
l.   1 3 2 5 8 7 3 5 6 1 2 5 3

Solfège

a.   d r m s l t d̄ t s l m r d
b.   m s l d r d̄ t l m s d r d̄
c.   s d d̄ t m r s l d d̄ s l m
d.   d̄ s l d r s m r s l d̄ t m
e.   d m r s l d̄ t m d r s l t
f.   m d r s l d d̄ t m s d m r
g.   s l d̄ t m d r s m r s d̄ t
h.   m s l d̄ d r d̄ t l m s m r
i.   m d r s l d̄ m d̄ t m r d s
j.   d̄ s l m r d d̄ t m d r s l
k.   m s l d d̄ t m r s d r d̄ s
l.   d m r s d̄ t m s l d r s m

Notes on the Staff

Tonic is on the first space below the staff.

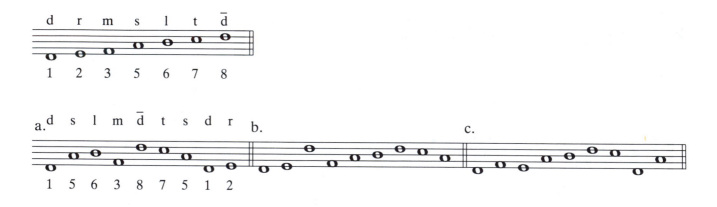

Melodies

Tonic is on the first space below the staff.

Tonic is in various positions.

65.

66.

Duets

67.

68.

m/3

Level 6 Exercises: scale degrees 1 2 3 4 5 6 7 8 / d r m f s l t d̄

Scale Degree Number

a. 1 2 3 5 4 8 7 5 6 3 1 2 5

b. 3 1 8 7 5 4 1 2 3 5 6 8 3

c. 5 6 3 4 8 7 1 2 5 3 4 8 5

d. 8 5 6 3 2 5 1 2 5 6 1 8 7

e. 5 3 1 2 8 7 5 4 1 3 5 6 3

f. 1 5 4 5 6 8 7 3 4 1 2 5 1

g. 3 4 5 1 2 8 7 5 6 3 2 8 7

h. 5 3 4 5 1 2 8 7 6 3 5 6 1

i. 8 5 6 3 2 1 8 7 3 4 1 5 6

j. 1 3 2 5 8 7 3 4 1 5 6 3 2

k. 5 3 4 8 7 5 6 1 2 5 3 2 8

l. 3 1 2 5 8 7 5 6 3 4 1 5 3

Solfège

a. d r m s f d̄ t s l m d r s

b. m d d̄ t s f d r m s l d̄ m

c. s l m f d̄ t d r s m f d̄ s

d. d̄ s l m r s d r s l d d̄ t

e. s m d r d̄ t s f d m s l m

f. d s f s l d̄ t m f d r s d

g. m f s d r d̄ t s l m r d̄ t

h. s m f s d r d̄ t l m s l d

i. d̄ s l m r d d̄ t m f d s l

j. d m r s d̄ t m f d s l m r

k. s m f d̄ t s l d r s m r d̄

l. m d r s d̄ t s l m f d s m

Notes on the Staff

Tonic is on the second line below the staff.

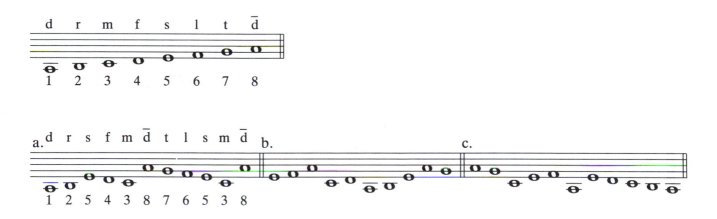

Melodies

Tonic is on the second line below the staff

Tonic is in various positions.

75.

76.

77.

Duets

78.

79.

m/3

Examples from the Literature

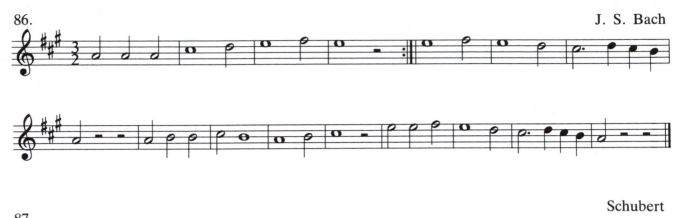

86.   J. S. Bach

Schubert

87.

RHYTHM

compound meter only;
undivided and divided beats (÷ 3)

PITCH

dominant to dominant

Rhythm

Compound Division: Division of the beat into three equal parts. For example, a dotted quarter may divide into three eighth notes.

Compound Meter: A meter in which the beat divides into three equal parts. In compound meter, the beat is always represented by a dotted note. Typical time signatures for compound meters are $\frac{3}{8}, \frac{3}{4}, \frac{6}{8}, \frac{6}{4}, \frac{9}{8}, \frac{12}{8}$. The guide for interpreting simple meter signatures (see Chapter 1) does not apply to compound meters. The upper number in a compound time signature indicates the number of beat *divisions* that together make up a measure. Thus in $\frac{6}{8}$, there are six eighth notes in the measure, but the measure is counted in two, each beat represented by a dotted quarter note.

Time signatures in which the upper number is 3, 6, 9, or 12 may have either a simple or a compound division of the beat, depending on the tempo. For example, a piece in $\frac{6}{8}$ in slow tempo is usually performed "in 6," that is, with six beats per measure and duple division of each beat (simple division). It becomes more practical in fast tempo to perform the same piece "in 2," that is, with two beats per measure and triple division of each beat (compound division). To determine the number of beats to tap for each measure in fast tempo with time signatures whose upper number is 3, 6, 9, or 12, divide the upper number of the time signature by three. (Thus, a piece in fast $\frac{12}{8}$ will be performed with four beats per measure, and each beat will have a triple division.)

54

Exercises without Ties

Exercises with Ties

17.

18.

19.

20.

Pitch (range: dominant to dominant)

Level 1 Exercises: scale degrees 5 6 7 8 / s l t d̄ (steps and skips)

Scale Degree Number

a. 5 6 7 8 7 5 6 5 8 7 6 8 5

b. 8 5 8 7 5 6 5 8 7 6 8 5 6

c. 5 6 5 8 5 8 7 5 6 8 7 6 8

d. 8 7 5 8 5 6 8 5 8 7 6 5 6

e. 5 6 5 8 7 5 6 8 5 8 7 5 8

f. 5 6 8 7 5 6 7 5 8 5 6 8 5

g. 5 8 7 5 6 8 5 6 8 7 5 6 7

h. 8 5 6 8 7 6 8 5 6 5 8 7 5

i. 5 8 7 5 6 5 8 5 6 7 5 8 7

j. 8 7 5 6 8 7 6 5 8 5 6 5 8

k. 5 8 7 5 8 7 6 5 6 5 8 7 5

l. 8 5 6 8 7 5 6 5 8 7 6 5 8

Solfège

a. s l t d̄ t s l s d̄ t l d̄ s

b. d̄ s d̄ t s l s d̄ t l d̄ s l

c. s l s d̄ s d̄ t s l d̄ t l d̄

d. d̄ t s d̄ s l d̄ s d̄ t l s l

e. s l s d̄ t s l d̄ s d̄ t s d̄

f. s l d̄ t s l t s d̄ s l d̄ s

g. s d̄ t s l d̄ s l d̄ t s l t

h. d̄ s l d̄ t l d̄ s l s d̄ t s

i. s d̄ t s l s d̄ s l t s d̄ t

j. d̄ t s l d̄ t l s d̄ s l s d̄

k. s d̄ t s d̄ t l s l s d̄ t s

l. d̄ s l d̄ t s l s d̄ t l s d̄

Notes on the Staff

Tonic is on the first space below the staff.

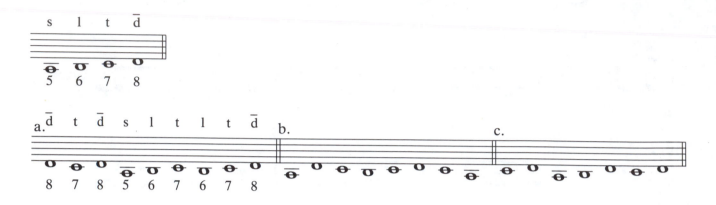

Melodies

Tonic is on the first space below the staff.

Tonic is in various positions.

Duets

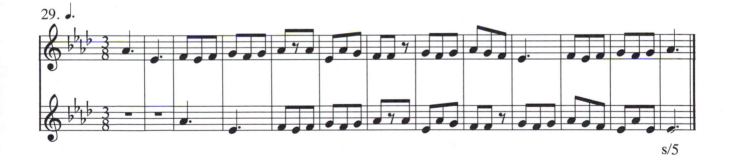

s/5

s/5

Level 2 Exercises: scale degrees 5̲ 1 3 5 / s̲ d m s

Note: Underlined scale degree numbers and solfège syllable letters represent pitches that sound below the tonic.

Scale Degree Number

a. 1 5̲ 1 3 5 1 5 3 1 5̲ 3 1 5
b. 3 1 5 5̲ 3 5 1 3 5̲ 5 1 3 5
c. 5 1 3 5̲ 3 5 1 5̲ 5 3 1 5 3
d. 5̲ 3 1 5 5̲ 1 5 1 3 5̲ 1 5 3
e. 3 1 5 5̲ 3 5 1 5̲ 5 3 1 5 3
f. 1 5 1 3 5̲ 1 5 3 5̲ 5 3 1 5̲
g. 5̲ 1 3 5 5̲ 3 5 1 5̲ 3 1 5 1
h. 3 5 1 3 5 3 1 5 3 5̲ 5 1 3
i. 3 1 5 5̲ 3 5 3 1 5̲ 3 5 1 5̲
j. 3 5 1 3 5 5̲ 1 5 3 5̲ 3 1 5
k. 5̲ 3 1 5 5̲ 3 1 5 3 5̲ 5 1 3
l. 5 1 3 5̲ 1 3 5 1 5 3 1 5̲ 1

Solfège

a. d s̲ d m s d s m d s̲ m d s
b. m d s s̲ m s d m s̲ s d m s
c. s d m s̲ m s d s̲ s m d s m
d. s̲ m d s s̲ d s d m s̲ d s m
e. m d s s̲ m s d s̲ s m d s m
f. d s d m s̲ d s m s̲ s m d s̲
g. s̲ d m s s̲ m s d s̲ m d s d
h. m s d m s m d s m s̲ s d m
i. m d s s̲ m s m d s̲ m s d s̲
j. m s d m s s̲ d s m s̲ m d s
k. s̲ m d s s̲ m d s m s̲ s d m
l. s d m s̲ d m s d s m d s̲ d

Notes on the Staff

Tonic is on the first space.

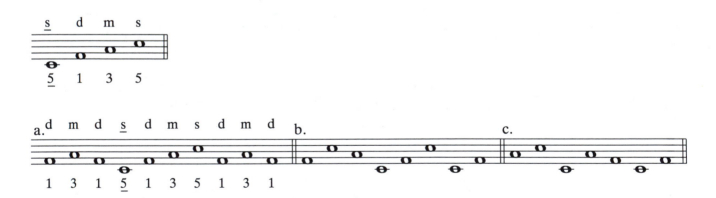

Melodies

Tonic is on the first space.

Tonic is in various positions.

37.

38.

Duets

39.

40.

Level 3 Exercises: scale degrees 5̲ 1 2 3 5 / s̲ d r m s

Scale Degree Number

a. 5̲ 1 3 2 5 3 5̲ 5 1 2 5 5̲ 3
b. 1 5 3 2 5̲ 3 1 2 5 3 5̲ 1 5
c. 3 1 3 5 5̲ 1 5̲ 3 1 2 5 3 2
d. 5 3 2 5̲ 5 1 3 5̲ 1 2 5 3 5̲
e. 1 5 3 2 5̲ 1 2 5̲ 3 5 1 3 5
f. 3 5 5̲ 1 5 3 2 5̲ 5 1 2 5 3
g. 3 5̲ 1 2 1 5 3 2 5̲ 3 1 5 5̲
h. 1 2 5̲ 3 5 3 2 5̲ 1 5 3 2 5̲
i. 3 5̲ 5 3 2 5 1 5̲ 1 2 5 3 2
j. 5̲ 3 2 1 5 5̲ 1 2 5 3 5̲ 3 5
k. 1 2 5 3 5̲ 3 2 5 1 2 5̲ 3 1
l. 5 5̲ 3 1 2 5 3 2 5̲ 1 3 5 1

Solfège

a. s̲ d m r s m s̲ s d r s s s̲ m
b. d s m r s̲ m d r s m s̲ d s
c. m d m s s̲ d s̲ m d r s m r
d. s m r s̲ s d m s̲ d r s m s̲
e. d s m r s d r s̲ m s d m s
f. m s s̲ d s m r s̲ s d r s m
g. m s̲ d r d s m r s̲ m d s s̲
h. d r s̲ m s m r s̲ d s m r s̲
i. m s̲ s m r s d s̲ d r s m r
j. s̲ m r d s s̲ d r s m s̲ m s
k. d r s m s̲ m r s d r s̲ m d
l. s s̲ m d r s m r s̲ d m s d

Notes on the Staff

Tonic is on the second space.

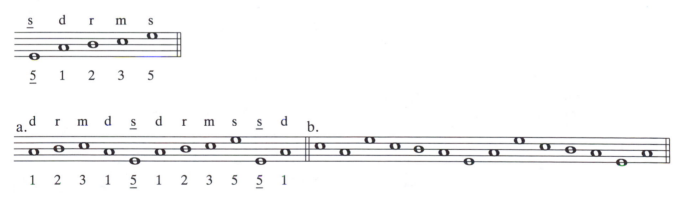

a. d r m d s̲ d r m s s̲ d b.

1 2 3 1 5̲ 1 2 3 5 5̲ 1

c.   d.

64   Chapter 3

Melodies

Tonic is on the second space.

Tonic is in various positions.

Duets

Level 4 Exercises: scale degrees 5̲ 6̲ 1 2 3 5 / s̲ l̲ d r m s

Scale Degree Number

a. 5̲ 6̲ 1 2 1 5 3 1 2 5̲ 6̲ 5 1
b. 3 5̲ 5 1 3 2 5̲ 6̲ 3 1 2 5 3
c. 1 5̲ 3 5 1 3 2 5̲ 6̲ 5 3 1 2
d. 5 3 1 2 5̲ 6̲ 5 3 5̲ 3 2 5̲ 1
e. 3 1 5 5̲ 6̲ 1 3 2 5̲ 5 1 2 3
f. 1 3 2 5̲ 5 5̲ 5̲ 6̲ 3 1 2 5 3 1
g. 3 1 5̲ 5 3 5̲ 6̲ 3 5 1 2 5 3
h. 5̲ 6̲ 3 2 5 1 2 5̲ 3 5 1 2 5̲
i. 5 3 2 5̲ 6̲ 1 2 5 1 3 5 5 3
j. 1 3 2 5̲ 6̲ 5 3 5̲ 1 2 5̲ 3 5
k. 3 5̲ 5 1 2 5̲ 6̲ 3 2 5 5̲ 3 1
l. 5̲ 3 2 5 1 5̲ 6̲ 1 3 2 5 1 2

Solfège

a. s̲ l̲ d r d s m d r s̲ l̲ s d
b. m s̲ s d m r s̲ l̲ m d r s m
c. d s̲ m s d m r s̲ l̲ s m d r
d. s m d r s̲ l̲ s m s̲ m r s̲ d
e. m d s s̲ l̲ d m r s̲ s d r m
f. d m r s̲ s s̲ l̲ m d r s m d
g. m d s̲ s m s l̲ m s d r s m
h. s̲ l̲ m r s d r s̲ m s d r s̲
i. s m r s̲ l̲ d r s d m s̲ s m
j. d m r s̲ l̲ s m s̲ d r s̲ m s
k. m s̲ s d r s̲ l̲ m r s s̲ m d
l. s̲ m r s d s̲ l̲ d m r s d r

Notes on the Staff

Tonic is on the third line.

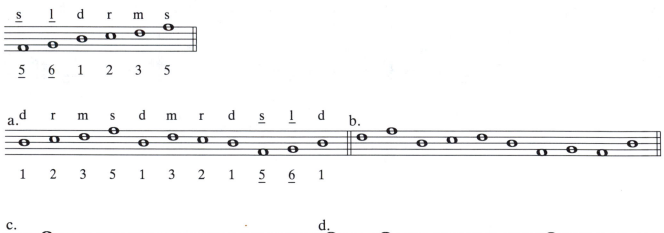

Melodies

Tonic is on the third line.

Tonic is in various positions.

58.

59.

Duets

60.

61.

Level 5 Exercises: scale degrees 5 6 7 1 2 3 5 / s l t d r m s

Scale Degree Number

a. 5 6 7 1 3 2 5 1 2 1 7 5 6
b. 1 2 5 3 2 5 6 1 7 5 1 5 3
c. 5 3 1 2 5 6 1 7 3 2 1 5 5
d. 3 2 5 6 7 5 1 2 5 3 5 3 2
e. 1 3 2 5 6 5 1 7 3 1 2 5 6
f. 5 3 1 2 5 5 6 1 7 3 2 5 3
g. 5 6 1 2 5 3 1 7 3 2 5 5 3
h. 5 1 2 5 6 3 2 5 1 7 6 3 2
i. 3 1 2 5 6 5 3 2 5 1 7 3 5
j. 1 3 2 5 5 6 3 1 7 5 3 1 2
k. 3 5 6 1 2 5 1 7 3 2 5 5 6
l. 5 3 2 5 6 1 5 1 2 1 7 6 3

Solfège

a. s l t d m r s d r d t s l
b. d r s m r s l d t s d s m
c. s m d r s l d t m r d s s
d. m r s l t s d r s m s m r
e. d m r s l s d t m d r s l
f. s m d r s s l d t m r s m
g. s l d r s m d t m r s s m
h. s d r s l m r s d t l m r
i. m d r s l s m r s d t m s
j. d m r s s l m d t s m d r
k. m s l d r s d t m r s s l
l. s m r s l d s d r d t l m

Notes on the Staff

Tonic is on the third space.

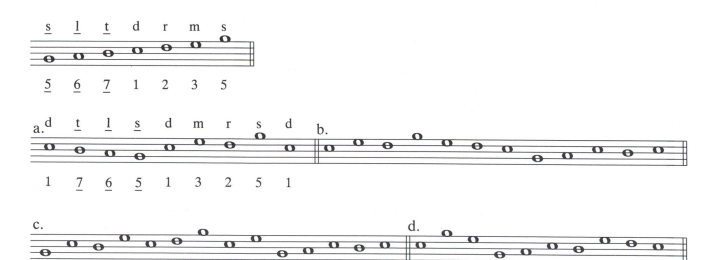

Melodies

Tonic is on the third space.

Tonic is in various positions.

Duets

m/3

Level 6 Exercises: scale degrees <u>5</u> <u>6</u> <u>7</u> 1 2 3 4 5 / <u>s</u> <u>l</u> <u>t</u> d r m f s

Scale Degree Number

a. <u>5</u> <u>6</u> <u>7</u> 1 5 4 1 2 3 <u>5</u> 1 <u>7</u> 3
b. 5 1 2 <u>5</u> <u>6</u> 3 1 <u>7</u> 3 4 1 5 3
c. 3 <u>5</u> <u>6</u> 5 4 3 1 <u>7</u> 3 2 <u>5</u> 1 2
d. 1 3 <u>5</u> <u>5</u> 4 3 <u>5</u> <u>6</u> 1 <u>7</u> <u>6</u> 3 2
e. 5 1 <u>7</u> 3 4 <u>5</u> <u>6</u> 3 2 5 1 2 <u>5</u>
f. 3 1 2 <u>5</u> <u>5</u> 4 5 <u>5</u> <u>6</u> 1 <u>7</u> 3 2
g. 3 <u>5</u> <u>6</u> 5 4 1 2 5 1 <u>7</u> <u>6</u> 3 5
h. 5 <u>5</u> <u>6</u> 3 2 1 3 4 1 <u>7</u> 5 1 2
i. 1 <u>7</u> 5 3 1 2 5 4 <u>5</u> <u>6</u> 3 1 5
j. <u>5</u> <u>6</u> 1 3 4 1 <u>7</u> 5 1 2 5 3 2
k. 3 5 <u>5</u> <u>6</u> 1 3 4 1 2 1 <u>7</u> <u>5</u> <u>6</u>
l. 1 5 <u>5</u> <u>6</u> 3 4 1 2 5 4 1 <u>7</u> 5

Solfège

a. <u>s</u> <u>l</u> <u>t</u> d s f d r m <u>s</u> d <u>t</u> m
b. s d r <u>s</u> <u>l</u> m d <u>t</u> m f d s m
c. m s <u>l</u> s f m d <u>t</u> m r <u>s</u> d r
d. d m <u>s</u> s f m <u>s</u> <u>l</u> d <u>t</u> <u>l</u> m r
e. s d <u>t</u> m f <u>s</u> <u>l</u> m r s d r <u>s</u>
f. m d r <u>s</u> s f s <u>s</u> <u>l</u> d <u>t</u> m r
g. m <u>s</u> <u>l</u> s f d r s d <u>t</u> <u>l</u> m s
h. s <u>s</u> <u>l</u> m r d m f d <u>t</u> s d r
i. d <u>t</u> s m d r s f <u>s</u> <u>l</u> m d s
j. <u>s</u> <u>l</u> d m f d <u>t</u> s d r s m r
k. m s <u>s</u> <u>l</u> d m f d r d <u>t</u> s <u>l</u>
l. d s <u>s</u> <u>l</u> m f d r s f d <u>t</u> <u>s</u>

Notes on the Staff

Tonic is on the fourth space.

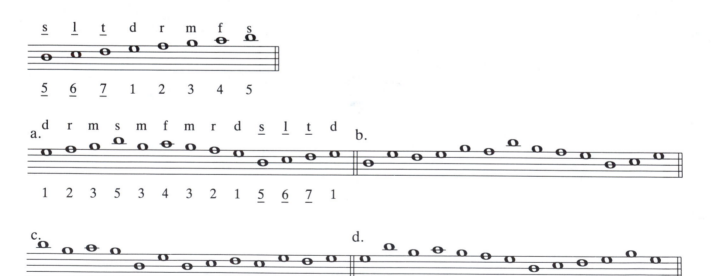

Melodies

Tonic is on the fourth space.

Tonic is in various positions.

78.

79.

80.

Duets

81.

m/3

82.

Examples from the Literature

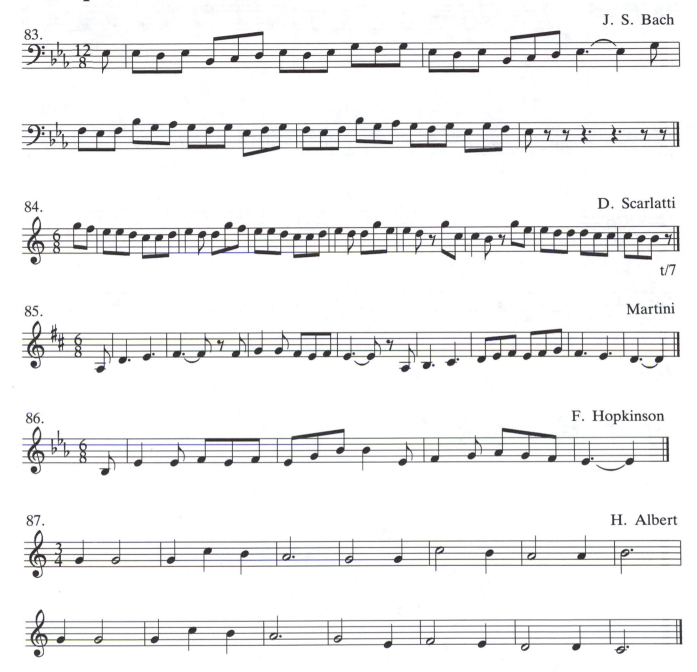

Tchaikovsky

88.

m/3

Hassler

89.

m/3

Haydn

90.

s/5

Chapter 4

SUMMARY OF PART I

RHYTHM

simple and compound meters;
undivided and divided beats
($\div 2$, $\div 3$), with ties

PITCH

tonic to tonic;
dominant to dominant

Rhythm Exercises

3.

4.

5.

6.

7.

8.

9.

10.

11.

12.

13.

14.

15.

16.

17.

18.

Pitch Exercises

Melodies

26.

27.

28.

29.

30.

31.

32.

33.

34.

35.

36.

37.

38.

39.

40.

41.

42.

43.

44.

45.

46.

47.

48.

49.

50.

51.

52.

53.

54.

Duets

55.

56.

57.

58.

59.

60.

61.

62.

Examples from the Literature

MINOR
KEYS

Chapter 5

RHYTHM

simple meter only;
subdivided beats (÷ 4), without ties

PITCH

tonic to tonic

Rhythm

Simple Subdivision: Just as the beat may be divided into two parts (simple division), the divisions of the beat in simple meter may be further divided, producing notes half the length of the divisions. For example, in $\frac{4}{4}$ the beat represented by a quarter note may be divided into two eighths, or subdivided into four sixteenths.

Preliminary Exercises

Repeat the pattern of each measure until it is
mastered before proceeding to the next measure.

1. The beat represented by ♩

2. The beat represented by ♪

3. The beat represented by 𝅗𝅥

Exercises

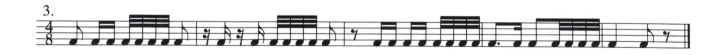

4.

5.

6.

7.

8.

9.

10.

11.

12.

13.

14.

15.

16.

17.

18.

19.

20.

Pitch (range: tonic to tonic)

The minor scale begins on the tonic and ascends for an octave. It employs some pitches that are different from those of the major scale and has a separate key signature. It resembles the major scale except for three scale degrees. The third scale degree is a half step lower than it is in the major scale, making the distance from 2 to 3 a half step and from 3 to 4 a whole step. This difference alone has a very great impact on the listener. The sixth scale degree is a half step above the fifth, and the seventh degree is a whole step below the tonic. This pattern is known as the *natural minor scale.* Compare the C major scale with the C natural minor scale.

C Natural Minor

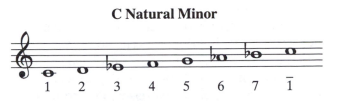

The symbols 3̬, 6̬, and 7̬ indicate the normal position of these scale degrees in the natural minor scale.

Although the natural minor scale is the basic form of the minor scale, the sixth and the seventh degrees sometimes occur in the same positions as they do in the major scale. These changes will appear in the music in the form of *accidentals* (sharps, flats, and naturals not in the key signature). In the Scale Degree Number exercises, these pitches are indicated by carets above the numbers (6̂, 7̂).

There are different approaches to learning the minor scales, and three different methods of assigning sight-singing syllables to the various scale degrees. Using the D minor scale as an example, we can illustrate these methods as follows:

C Major

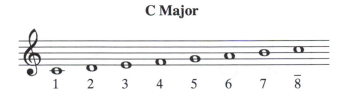

1	2	3̬	4	5	6̂	7̂	8	7̬	6̬	5	4	3̬	2	1
la	ti	do	re	mi	fi	si	la	sol	fa	mi	re	do	ti	la
do	re	me	fa	sol	la	ti	do	te	le	sol	fa	me	re	do

Your teacher may indicate a preference for one method over the others. Each approach has some advantages and some disadvantages, but the final goal is improving your sight-singing ability. Singing the correct syllable or number is less important than singing the correct pitch.

Because of the variety of syllable systems used for minor keys, only the scale degree numbers will be used in Part II of this book; no solfège syllables will be indicated. Similarly, only scale degree numbers will be used for scale degree exercises, for Notes on the Staff exercises, and to indicate the final pitch of melodies that do not end on the tonic.

Following are Scale Degree Number exercises using minor scales. To distinguish the third, sixth, and seventh scale degree numbers from their major scale counterparts, carets will be used in conjunction with the numbers representing these scale degrees. Thus, a downward caret under the number 3 (3̬) indicates that the third scale degree

is in its minor scale form, that is, it sounds a half step above scale degree 2. A downward caret under the number 6 (6̬) indicates that the sixth scale degree is to sound a half step above the fifth scale degree and a caret under the number 7 (7̬) indicates that the seventh scale degree is to sound a whole step below the eighth scale degree. An upward caret above the number 6̂ indicates that the sixth scale degree is to sound a whole step above the fifth scale degree and an upward caret above the number 7̂ indicates that the seventh scale degree is to sound a half step below the eighth scale degree. Similarly, in the Notes on the Staff exercises that follow, carets are placed above or below notes which represent the third, sixth, and seventh scale degrees with the same application as in the Scale Degree Number exercises.

The Melodies and Duets sections of each level of exercises use simple and compound meters, divided beats ($\div 2$, $\div 3$), ties, and subdivided beats ($\div 4$) on repeated pitches only.

Level 1 Exercises: scale degrees 1 3̬ 5 8

Scale Degree Number

a. 1 3̬ 5 8 5 1 3̬ 8 3̬ 8 1 8 5

b. 8 5 1 3̬ 5 1 8 3̬ 5 8 3̬ 5 1

c. 3̬ 5 1 8 5 1 3̬ 8 1 5 3̬ 8 3̬

d. 8 3̬ 5 1 3̬ 8 5 1 5 8 3̬ 8 1

e. 5 3̬ 8 1 3̬ 5 1 8 3̬ 8 5 1 5

f. 3̬ 8 1 5 3̬ 1 8 5 3̬ 5 8 1 3̬

g. 3̬ 1 8 3̬ 5 3̬ 8 1 3̬ 5 1 8 3̬

h. 5 1 5 8 3̬ 8 1 5 3̬ 1 8 3̬ 5

i. 8 1 3̬ 8 5 1 5 8 3̬ 1 5 3̬ 8

j. 3̬ 8 3̬ 5 1 8 3̬ 1 5 8 1 5 3̬

k. 1 5 3̬ 8 5 3̬ 8 1 5 3̬ 1 5 8

l. 5 8 1 8 3̬ 8 3̬ 1 5 8 5 3̬ 1

Notes on the Staff

Tonic is on the first space.

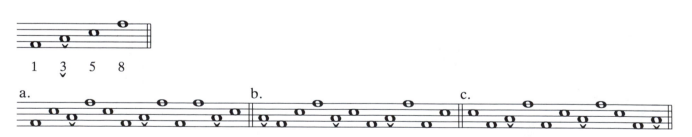

Melodies

Tonic is on the first space.

In these exercises, major as well as minor keys are used, so you must determine the key and the location of the tonic on the staff before you begin. Often, the final pitch of the phrase will be the tonic, but it may also be the third or the fifth scale degree or, less often, the second or the seventh degree.

27.

28.

29.

30.

31.

32.

Duets

33.

34.

Level 2 Exercises: scale degrees 1 2 3̌ 5 8

Scale Degree Number

a.   1 2 3̌ 5 8 1 3̌ 2 8 1 5 3̌ 2
b.   3̌ 2 5 1 2 8 5 3̌ 8 1 5 3̌ 8
c.   1 5 3̌ 2 8 1 5 1 2 8 3̌ 2 5
d.   5 8 1 3̌ 2 5 1 2 8 3̌ 5 1 2
e.   3̌ 2 8 5 1 2 3̌ 8 1 5 3̌ 2 8
f.   1 3̌ 5 8 1 3̌ 2 1 5 1 2 3̌ 8

g.   3̌ 2 8 5 1 5 1 2 8 3̌ 1 2 5
h.   1 5 3̌ 2 8 1 2 5 8 3̌ 1 5 3̌
i.   3̌ 8 5 1 2 5 3̌ 2 8 3̌ 2 5 1
j.   5 3̌ 2 5 8 1 2 3̌ 1 8 3̌ 2 5
k.   3̌ 5 1 2 8 1 3̌ 2 5 8 1 5 3̌
l.   8 5 3̌ 2 5 1 2 8 3̌ 5 1 2 8

Notes on the Staff

Tonic is on the first line below the staff.

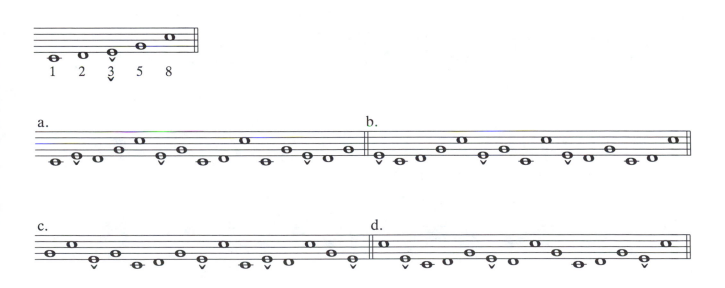

Melodies

Tonic is on the first line below the staff.

35.

Tonic is in various positions.

39.

40.

41.

42.

43.

44.

45.

46.

Duets

47.
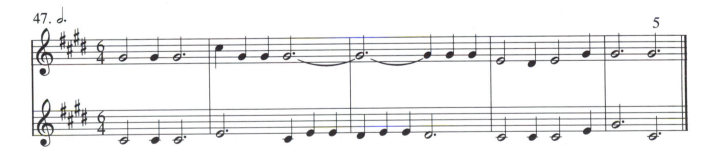

3

Level 3 Exercises: scale degrees 1 2 3̬ 5 6̬ 8

Scale Degree Number

a. 1 2 3̬ 5 6̬ 8 5 3̬ 2 5 1 2 8

b. 3̬ 1 2 5 6̬ 1 8 3̬ 2 5 8 5 6̬

c. 5 6̬ 1 8 3̬ 2 8 1 5 1 5 6̬ 3̬

d. 1 5 3̬ 2 8 1 5 6̬ 3̬ 1 2 5 6̬

e. 5 6̬ 8 1 3̬ 2 5 1 2 5 6̬ 8 3̬

f. 3̬ 5 1 8 5 6̬ 1 3̬ 2 1 2 5 6̬

g. 1 5 6̬ 3̬ 2 8 1 2 5 6̬ 8 3̬ 2

h. 5 3̬ 1 2 8 5 6̬ 3 8 3̬ 2 1 5

i. 8 3̬ 5 6̬ 3̬ 1 2 5 3̬ 2 8 5 6̬

j. 3̬ 2 5 1 8 5 6̬ 1 2 5 3̬ 8 1

k. 5 6̬ 8 3̬ 2 5 1 2 8 5 6̬ 3̬ 2

l. 1 3̬ 2 5 6̬ 8 3̬ 1 2 8 5 6̬ 3̬

Notes on the Staff

Tonic is on the first space below the staff.

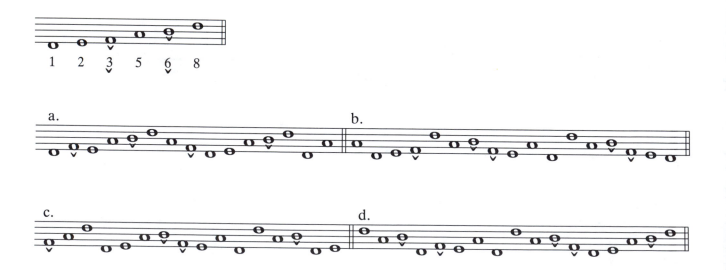

Melodies

Tonic is on the first space below the staff.

Tonic is in various positions.

55.

56.

57.

58.

59.

Duets

60.

5

61.

Level 4 Exercises: scale degrees 1 2 3 5 6 7 8

Scale Degree Number

a. 1 2 3 5 6 7 8 7 5 6 3 2 1   g. 5 6 8 7 3 1 2 5 3 2 5 8 7

b. 3 5 6 1 2 8 7 6 3 5 1 2 8   h. 3 5 6 8 1 2 8 7 6 3 5 3 2

c. 5 1 8 7 3 2 5 6 1 8 5 6 3   i. 3 1 2 5 6 8 3 8 7 3 2 1 5

d. 8 5 6 1 2 5 3 2 5 6 8 1 3   j. 8 5 6 3 2 1 8 7 3 1 2 5 6

e. 1 3 2 5 6 8 7 3 1 2 5 6 7   k. 3 5 6 1 8 7 3 2 5 1 2 8 5

f. 3 1 2 5 6 1 8 7 3 5 1 3 2   l. 1 3 2 5 8 7 3 5 6 1 2 5 3

Notes on the Staff

Tonic is on the second line.

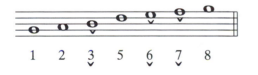

1   2   3   5   6   7   8

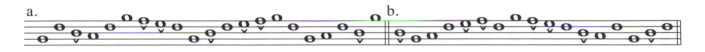

a.   b.

c.   d.

Melodies

Tonic is on the second line.

Tonic is in various positions.

69.

70.

71.

72.

Duets

73.

74.

Examples from the Literature

Chapter 6

RHYTHM

compound meter only;
subdivided beats (÷ 6), without ties

PITCH

tonic to tonic

Rhythm

Compound Subdivision: The divisions of the beat in compound meter may be further divided, producing notes one-half the length of the divisions. For example, in ⁶⁄₈ the beat, which is represented by the dotted quarter, may be divided into three eighths, or subdivided into six sixteenths.

Preliminary Exercises

1. The beat represented by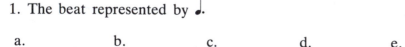

2. The beat represented by ♪.

3. The beat represented by ♩.

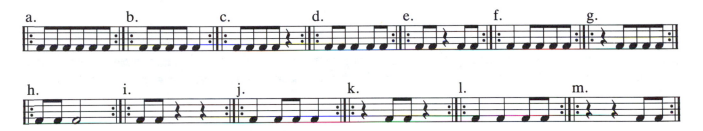

Exercises

3.

4.

5.

6.

7.

8.

9.

10.

11.

12.

13.

14.

15.

16.

17.

18.
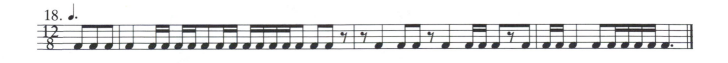

19.

20.

Exercises Including Materials Studied Previously

21.

22.

23.

24.

25.

26.

27.

28.

29.

30.

31.

32.

33.

34.

Pitch (range: tonic to tonic)

The Melodies and Duets sections of each level of exercises use simple and compound meters, divided beats (÷ 2, ÷ 3), ties, and subdivided beats (÷ 6) on repeated pitches only.

Level 1 Exercises: natural minor

Scale Degree Number

a. 1 3 2 5 4 8 7 5 6 3 1 2 5

b. 3 1 8 7 5 4 1 2 3 5 6 8 3

c. 5 6 3 4 8 7 1 2 5 3 4 8 5

d. 8 5 6 3 2 5 1 2 5 6 1 8 7

e. 5 3 1 2 8 7 5 4 1 3 5 6 3

f. 1 5 4 5 6 8 7 3 4 1 2 5 1

g. 3 4 5 1 2 8 7 5 6 3 2 8 7

h. 5 3 4 5 1 2 8 7 6 3 5 6 1

i. 8 5 6 3 2 1 8 7 3 4 1 5 6

j. 1 3 2 5 8 7 3 4 1 5 6 3 2

k. 5 3 4 8 7 5 6 1 2 5 3 2 8

l. 3 1 2 5 8 7 5 6 3 4 1 5 3

Notes on the Staff

Tonic is on the first line.

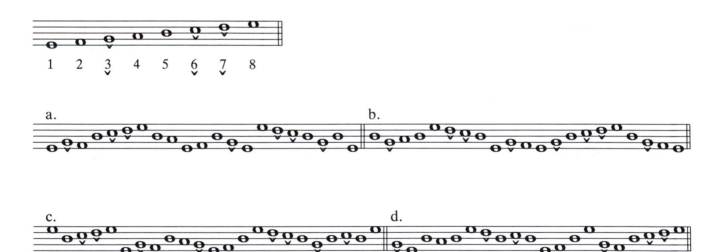

1   2   3   4   5   6   7   8

Melodies

Tonic is on the first line.

Tonic is in various positions.

42.

43.

44.

45.

Duets

46.

47.

Level 2 Exercises

Solo/Ensemble Scale Degree Number

These exercises emphasize the variable sixth and seventh scale degrees. Each number or dash represents a beat. Repeat each exercise until it is mastered before proceeding to the next exercise.

```
        solo ─────────┐ ensemble ──────┐              solo ─────────┐ ensemble ──────┐
a.  1 2 3̬ 5 3̬ 5 8 – 8 7̬ 6̬ 5 5 – – –          e.  5 6̂ 7̂ 5 8 5 5 – 8 7̬ 6̬ 5 5 – – –
b.  1 3̬ 2 5 8 5 1 – 8 7̬ 6̬ 5 5 – – –          f.  3̬ 5 6̂ 7̂ 8 5 5 – 8 7̬ 6̬ 5 5 – – –
c.  1 3̬ 5 8 5 3̬ 1 – 8 7̬ 6̬ 5 5 – – –          g.  5 6̂ 7̂ 5 6̂ 7̂ 8 – 8 7̬ 6̬ 5 5 – – –
d.  1 2 3 5 6̂ 7̂ 8 – 8 7̬ 6̬ 5 5 – – –          h.  1 3̬ 2 3̬ 5 6̂ 7̂ – 8 7̬ 6̬ 5 5 – – –
```

Scale Degree Number

```
a.  1 5 6̂ 7̂ 8 5 8 7̬ 6̬ 5 3̬ 4 1             g.  8 7̬ 6̬ 5 3̬ 1 2 5 6̂ 7̂ 5 8 7̂
b.  5 3̬ 5 8 7̬ 6̬ 5 1 5 6̂ 7̂ 8 5             h.  3̬ 5 6̬ 5 4 1 2 8 7̬ 6̬ 5 6̂ 7̂
c.  3̬ 5 8 7̬ 6̬ 5 6̬ 1 5 6̂ 7̂ 5 3̬           i.  1 2 5 3̬ 5 6̂ 7̂ 5 8 7̬ 6̬ 8 5
d.  8 5 6̂ 7̂ 8 3̬ 4 5 8 7̬ 6̬ 5 1             j.  5 3̬ 5 8 7̬ 6̬ 5 1 3̬ 5 6̂ 7̂ 8
e.  3̬ 5 6̂ 5 6̂ 7̂ 8 5 8 7̬ 6̬ 8 5            k.  1 3̬ 2 5 6̂ 7̂ 5 8 7̬ 6̬ 5 3̬ 2
f.  5 1 8 7̬ 6̬ 5 3̬ 5 6̬ 5 6̂ 7̂ 8            l.  8 5 6̂ 5 3̬ 4 5 6̂ 7̂ 8 5 3̬ 1
```

Notes on the Staff

Tonic is on the second line below the staff.

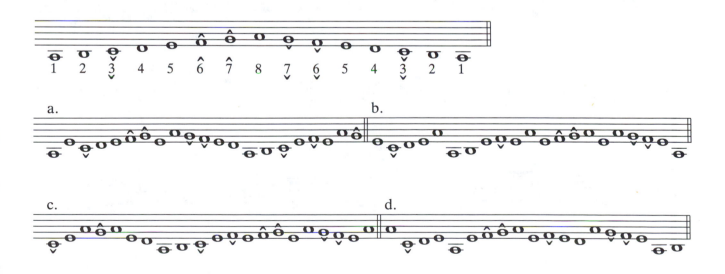

Melodies

Tonic is on the second line below the staff.

Tonic is in various positions.

55.

56.

57.

58.

59.

Duets

60.

61.

Examples from the Literature

65.

Handel

5

66.

Schubert

3

67.

Lassus

68.

M. Franck

69.

J. S. Bach

70.   Spiritual

71.   Hassler

Chapter 7

RHYTHM

simple meter only;
subdivided beats (÷ 4), with ties

PITCH

dominant to dominant

Rhythm

Preliminary Exercises

1. The beat represented by ♩

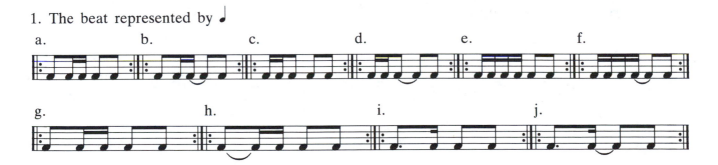

2. The beat represented by ♪

a. b. c. d. e. f.

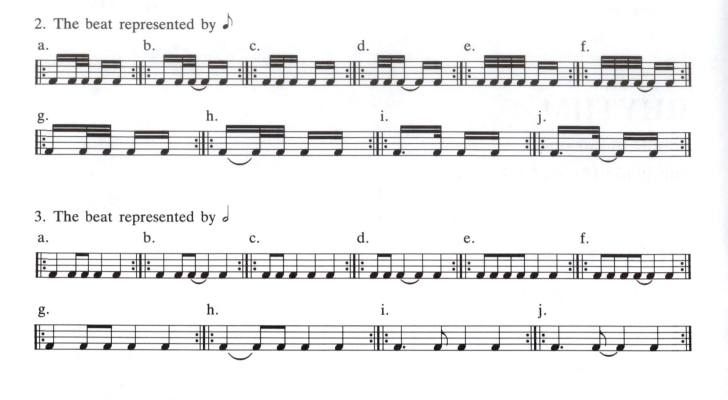

g. h. i. j.

3. The beat represented by ♩

a. b. c. d. e. f.

g. h. i. j.

Exercises

1.

2. ♪

3.

4.

14.

15.

16.

Exercises Including Materials Studied Previously

17.

18.

19.

20.

21.

22.

23.

24.

25.

26.

27.

28.

29.

30.

Pitch (range: dominant to dominant)

The Melodies and Duets sections of each level of exercises use simple and compound meters, divided beats ($\div 2$, $\div 3$), with ties, and subdivided beats ($\div 4$) on repeated pitches only.

Level 1 Exercises: scale degrees 5 1 3 5

Note: An underlined scale degree number represents a pitch that sounds *below* the tonic.

Scale Degree Number

a. 1 5 1 3 5 1 5 3 1 5 3 1 5
b. 3 1 5 5 3 5 1 3 5 5 1 3 5
c. 5 1 3 5 3 5 1 5 5 3 1 5 3
d. 5 3 1 5 5 1 5 1 3 5 1 5 3
e. 3 1 5 5 3 5 1 5 5 3 1 5 3
f. 1 5 1 3 5 1 5 3 5 5 3 1 5

g. 5 1 3 5 5 3 5 1 5 3 1 5 1
h. 3 5 1 3 5 3 1 5 3 5 5 1 3
i. 3 1 5 5 3 5 3 1 5 3 5 1 5
j. 3 5 5 1 5 3 1 5 3 5 1 5 3
k. 5 3 1 5 5 3 1 5 3 5 5 1 3
l. 5 1 3 5 1 3 5 1 5 3 1 5 1

Notes on the Staff

Tonic is on the third space.

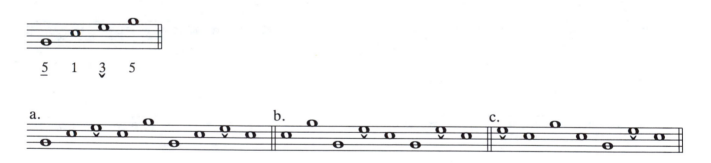

5   1   3   5

Melodies

Tonic is on the third space.

31.

Tonic is in various positions.

40.

41.

Duets

42.

43.

Level 2 Exercises: scale degrees 5̲ 1 2 3̬ 5

Scale Degree Number

a. 5̲ 1 3̬ 2 5 3̬ 5̲ 5 1 2 5 5̲ 3̬   g. 3̬ 5̲ 1 2 1 5 3̬ 2 5̲ 3̬ 1 5 5̲

b. 1 5 3̬ 2 5̲ 3̬ 1 2 5 3̬ 5̲ 1 5   h. 1 2 5̲ 3̬ 5 3̬ 2 5̲ 1 5 3̬ 2 5̲

c. 3̬ 1 3̬ 5 5̲ 1 5̲ 3̬ 1 2 5 3̬ 2   i. 3̬ 5̲ 5 3̬ 2 5 1 5̲ 1 2 5 3̬ 2

d. 5 3̬ 2 5̲ 5 1 3̬ 5̲ 1 2 5 3̬ 5̲   j. 5̲ 3̬ 2 1 5 5̲ 1 2 5 3̬ 5̲ 3̬ 5

e. 1 5 3̬ 2 5̲ 1 2 5̲ 3̬ 5 1 3̬ 5   k. 1 2 5 3̬ 5̲ 3̬ 2 5 1 2 5̲ 3̬ 1

f. 3̬ 5 5̲ 1 5 3̬ 2 5̲ 5 1 2 5 3̬   l. 5 5̲ 3̬ 1 2 5 3̬ 2 5 1 3̬ 5 1

Notes on the Staff

Tonic is on the fourth space.

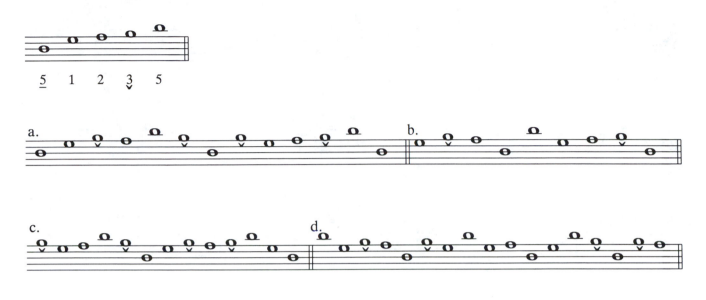

Melodies

Tonic is on the fourth space.

Tonic is in various positions.

Duets

Level 3 Exercises: scale degrees 5̲ 6̲ 1 2 3̲ 5

Scale Degree Number

a. 5̲ 6̲ 1 2 1 5 3̲ 1 2 5̲ 6̲ 5 1

b. 3̲ 5̲ 5 1 3̲ 2 5̲ 6̲ 3 1 2 5 3̲

c. 1 5̲ 3̲ 5 1 3̲ 2 5̲ 6̲ 5 3̲ 1 2

d. 5 3̲ 1 2 5̲ 6̲ 5 3̲ 5̲ 3̲ 2 5̲ 1

e. 3̲ 1 5 5̲ 6̲ 1 3̲ 2 5̲ 5 1 2 3̲

f. 1 3̲ 2 5̲ 5 5̲ 6̲ 3̲ 1 2 5 3̲ 1

g. 3̲ 1 5̲ 5 3̲ 5̲ 6̲ 3̲ 5 1 2 5 3̲

h. 5̲ 6̲ 3̲ 2 5 1 2 5̲ 3̲ 5 1 2 5̲

i. 5 3̲ 2 5̲ 6̲ 1 2 5 1 3̲ 5̲ 5 3̲

j. 1 3̲ 2 5̲ 6̲ 5 3̲ 5̲ 1 2 5̲ 3̲ 5

k. 3̲ 5̲ 5 1 2 5̲ 6̲ 3̲ 2 5 5̲ 3̲ 1

l. 5̲ 3̲ 2 5 1 5̲ 6̲ 1 3̲ 2 5 1 2

Notes on the Staff

Tonic is on the first space.

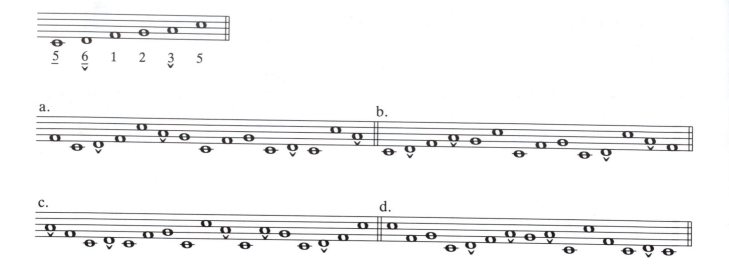

Melodies

Tonic is on the first space.

61.

Tonic is in various positions.

62.

63.

64.

65.

66.

67.

68.

Duets

69.

70.

5

Level 4 Exercises: scale degrees 5̲ 6̲ 7̂ 1 2 3̌ 5

Scale Degree Number

a. 5̲ 6̲ 1 3̌ 2 5 3̌ 1 7̂ 5̲ 6̲ 1 2

b. 3̌ 1 2 5 3̌ 1 7̂ 5̲ 6̲ 1 3̌ 2 5

c. 1 5 3̌ 1 2 5̲ 6̲ 1 7̂ 1 3̌ 2 5

d. 5 3̌ 5̲ 1 7̂ 5̲ 6̲ 5 3̌ 1 2 5 3̌

e. 1 2 5 3̌ 5 5̲ 6̲ 1 7̂ 5̲ 3̌ 1 2

f. 3̌ 1 2 5̲ 5 1 7̂ 5̲ 6̲ 5 3̌ 5̲ 1

g. 1 3̌ 2 5 5̲ 1 7̂ 5̲ 6̲ 5̲ 1 2 5

h. 3̌ 2 5 5̲ 6̲ 5 1 7̂ 5̲ 1 3̌ 5 1

i. 5 1 2 5 1 3̌ 5̲ 6̲ 1 7̂ 1 3̌ 5

j. 3̌ 1 5 5̲ 3̌ 1 7̂ 5̲ 6̲ 1 3̌ 2 1

k. 5̲ 3̌ 5 1 7̂ 5 1 5̲ 6̲ 3̌ 2 1 5

l. 1 3̌ 5̲ 1 2 5 1 7̂ 5̲ 6̲ 3̌ 2 1

Notes on the Staff

Tonic is on the first space below the staff.

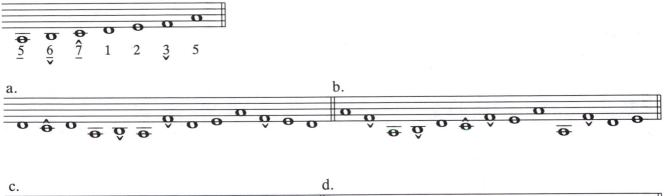

Melodies

Tonic is on the first space below the staff.

Tonic is in various positions.

Duets

Level 5 Exercises: 5̲ 6̲ 7̲ 1 2 3 5

Scale Degree Number

a. 5̲ 6̲ 7̲ 1 3 2 5 1 2 1 7̲ 5̲ 6̲

b. 1 2 5 3 2 5̲ 6̲ 1 7̲ 5 1 5̲ 3

c. 5 3 1 2 5̲ 6̲ 1 7̲ 3 2 1 5 5̲

d. 3 2 5̲ 6̲ 7̲ 5 1 2 5 3 5̲ 3 2

e. 1 3 2 5̲ 6̲ 5 1 7̲ 3 1 2 5̲ 6̲

f. 5̲ 3 1 2 5 5̲ 6̲ 1 7̲ 3 2 5̲ 3

g. 5̲ 6̲ 1 2 5 3 1 7̲ 3 2 5̲ 5 3

h. 5 1 2 5̲ 6̲ 3 2 5 1 7̲ 6̲ 3 2

i. 3 1 2 5̲ 6̲ 5 3 2 5̲ 1 7̲ 3 5

j. 1 3 2 5 5̲ 6̲ 3 1 7̲ 5 3 1 2

k. 3 5̲ 6̲ 1 2 5 1 7̲ 3 2 5 5̲ 6̲

l. 5 3 2 5̲ 6̲ 1 5 1 2 1 7̲ 6̲ 3

Notes on the Staff

Tonic is on the second space.

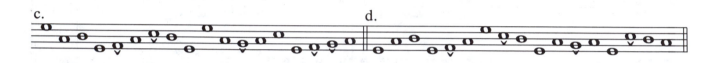

5 6 7 1 2 3 5

a.
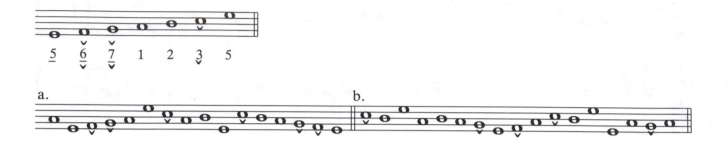
b.

c.
d.

Melodies

Tonic is on the second space.

84.

85.

86.

87.

88.

Tonic is in various positions.

89.

90.

91.

92.

93.

94.

95.

Duets

96.

97.

5

Examples from the Literature

98.   Hassler

5

99.   Schubert

5

100.   Beethoven

Chapter **8**

RHYTHM

compound meter only;
subdivided beats (÷ 6), with ties

PITCH

dominant to dominant

Rhythm

Preliminary Exercises

1. The beat represented by ♩.

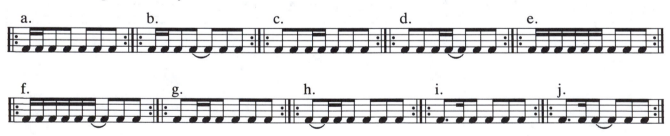

2. The beat represented by ♪.

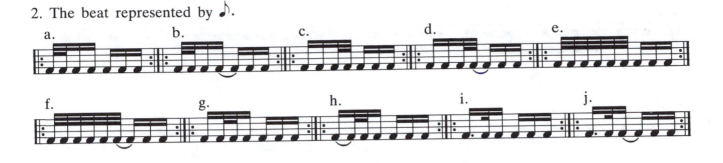

3. The beat represented by ♩.

Exercises

1.

2.

3.

4.

5.

6.

7.

8.

9.

10.

11.

12.

13.

14.

15.

16.

17.

18.

19.

Exercises Including Materials Studied Previously

Pitch (range: dominant to dominant)

The Melodies and Duets sections of each level of exercises use simple and compound meters, and divided beats (÷2, ÷3), with ties.

Level 1 Exercises: natural minor scale

Scale Degree Number

a. 5 6 7 1 5 1 2 3 5 1 7 3 2

b. 5 1 2 5 6 3 1 7 3 4 1 5 3

c. 3 5 6 5 4 3 1 7 3 2 5 1 2

d. 1 3 5 5 4 3 5 6 1 7 6 3 2

e. 5 1 7 3 4 5 6 3 2 5 1 2 5

f. 3 1 2 5 5 4 5 5 6 1 7 3 2

g. 3 5 6 5 4 1 2 5 1 7 6 3 5

h. 5 5 6 3 2 1 3 4 1 7 5 1 2

i. 1 7 5 3 1 2 5 4 5 6 3 1 5

j. 5 6 1 3 4 1 7 5 1 2 5 3 2

k. 3 5 5 6 1 3 4 1 2 1 7 5 6

l. 1 5 5 6 3 4 1 2 5 4 1 7 5

Notes on the Staff

Tonic is on the first space.

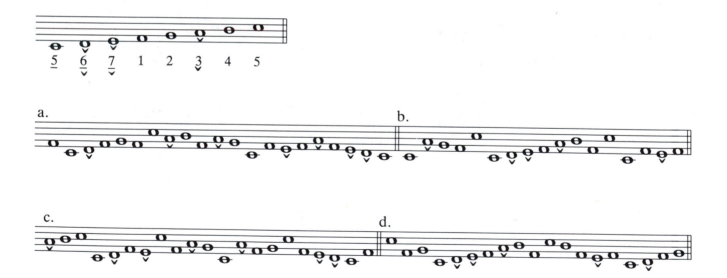

Melodies

Tonic is on the first space.

Tonic is in various positions.

42.

43.

44.

45.

46.

Duets

47.

5

Level 2 Exercises

Scale Degree Number

a. 5 6̂ 7̂ 5 1 7 6 5 3 1 2 5 1

b. 3 5 4 1 2 5 6 5 6̂ 7̂ 1 2 5

c. 3 1 7 6 5 1 7̂ 1 5 3 4 1 5

d. 5 3 2 5 6̂ 7̂ 5 1 7 6 5 3 2

e. 1 3 4 5 5 6̂ 7̂ 5 1 7 6 5 1

f. 5 6 5 1 7̂ 1 2 5 6 7 1 3 5

g. 3 1 7 6 5 1 7̂ 1 3 4 5 1 2

h. 1 3 2 5 4 1 7 6 5 6̂ 1 7̂ 1

i. 5 1 2 5 6̂ 7̂ 5 1 7 6 5 3 2

j. 3 5 4 1 2 1 7 6 5 6̂ 7̂ 5 1

k. 1 3 5 4 3 1 7 6 5 3 2 5 1

l. 3 1 2 5 4 1 7 6 5 1 5 6̂ 7̂

Notes on the Staff

Tonic is on the fourth space.

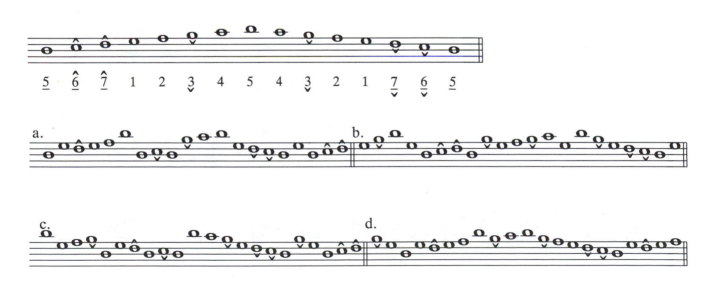

Melodies

Tonic is on the fourth space.

Tonic is in various positions.

56.

57.

58.

59.

Duets

60.

61.

Examples from the Literature

62.   Hassler

63.   Hassler

64.   Vittoria

65.   Schubert

2

66.   Hausmann

67.   Schubert

68.   J. S. Bach

5

69.   J. S. Bach

5

70.   Schubert

71.   J. S. Bach

5

SUMMARY OF PART II

RHYTHM

simple and compound meters;
subdivided beats (÷ 4, ÷ 6),
with ties

PITCH

dominant to dominant;
tonic to tonic

Rhythm Exercises

3.

4.

5.

6.

7.

8.

9.

10.

11.

12.

13.

14.

15.

16.

17.

18.

19.

20.

21.

22.

23.

24.

25.

26.

27.

28.

Pitch Exercises

Melodies

37.

38.

39.

40.

41.

42.

2

43.

44.

45.

46.

47.

48.

49.

2

50.

51.

52.

53.

5

54.

55.

56.

57.

58.

5

59.

60.

61.

62.

63.

64.

65.

66.

67.

68.

69.

70.

71.

72.

73.

74.

Duets

75.

76.

77.

78.

79.

80.

81.

82.

Examples from the Literature

Hassler

83.

3

84.

Hassler

Part **III**

SUPPLEMENTARY EXERCISES

Chapter 10

ADDITIONAL EXERCISES IN MAJOR AND MINOR KEYS

Rhythm Exercises

5.

6.

7.

8.

9.

10.

11.

12.

13.

14.

15.

16.

17.

18.

19.

20.

Pitch Exercises

Melodies

29.

30.

31.

32.

33.

34.

35.

36.

37.

38.

39.

40.

41.

42.

43.

44.

45.
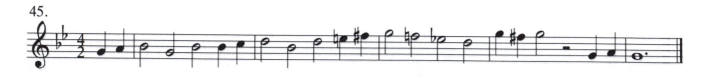

46.

Duets

47.

5

48.

49.

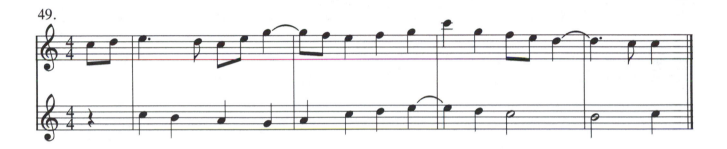

50.

51.

52.

53.

54.

Examples from the Literature